talking the boundless book

art, language, and the book arts

talking the boundless book

art, language, and the book arts

essays from

Art & Language: Re-Reading the Boundless Book

a Minnesota Center for Book Arts Symposium

Dick Higgins, Steven Clay, Johanna Drucker, Charles Bernstein, Amos Paul Kennedy, Jr., Susan Bee, Toshi Ishihara & Linda Reinfeld, Katherine Kuehn, Jo Anne Paschall, Colette Gaiter, Alison Knowles, Byron Clercx, Brad Freeman, Karen Wirth

edited & introduced by Charles Alexander

minnesota center for book arts

minneapolis, minnesota 1995

Minnesota Center for Book Arts
24 North Third Street
Minneapolis, Minnesota 55401

Printed in the United States of America
International Standard Book Number: 1-879832-09-7
Library of Congress Catalog Card Number 95-81013

Book Design by Charles Alexander
Cover Design by Blake Bakken with image by Colette Gaiter

Manufactured in the United States of America
First edition

Minnesota Center for Book Arts is grateful for the voluntary
services of several people who helped make this book possible:

Kari Andruscavage	Barbara Harman
Blake Bakken	Rebecca Hunt
Carolyn Carlson	Eliza Murphy
Tina M. Cassler	Michelle Smith

This book is part of a project that includes an exhibition and
symposium and is titled *Art & Language: Re-Reading the
Boundless Book,* made possible in part by funds from the National
Endowment for the Arts Visual Arts Program.

Perhaps we have been the moment when the book turns on its thirst.

But who would have opened it, this book? How did we enter, caught in our own trap? And for what reading have we been alphabet?

What use to worry about our daring? Man will forever be read. The question writes us.

–Edmond Jabès

table of contents

Introduction

Charles Alexander

Like notions of self, author, and reader, book is not a word which lends itself to easy definition. The book arts, perhaps, are specifically arguments against definition and limitation, as artists and writers strive to break the bindings of what has traditionally been considered a book. Such work has taken place in an arena which has not yet cast a discerning eye on itself; a fledgling field, this book arts place, albeit one which involves traditions going back to some of the first activities of humankind, keeping records by making marks on stones, clay, and other surfaces. Book arts works today are made by visual artists, writers, publishers, and others; they are collected by libraries and museums, displayed by museums and galleries; they are taught in colleges and universities as well as in community education programs.

Book arts criticism is a child. A handful of columns in magazines, a few journals, some exhibition catalogs, one major anthology, and little else. Most of the publications in the field are "how-to" books on bookbinding, papermaking, and letterpress printing. They encourage the practice, extension, and development of traditional crafts; yet the work of many artists in the field of the book arts is more holistic — it involves a wholescale approach to the book as artistic possibility, with consideration of history, aesthetic and cultural theory, social aspects of art making, poetics, and economics. It can even be, in certain hands, an assault on the hegemonic tendencies of the commerce of the book in a post-capitalist era. It is, in short, at the forefront of what art is, what it means, and what it might come to mean, and it accomplishes this work in a format which provides an intimate, one-to-one interaction between art work and audience. A craft-based criticism, while essential in its own right, embraces only a small part of what is called for. It is time for more, but where does one begin?

At Minnesota Center for Book Arts we began by inviting fifteen artists to convene over three days to discuss the book arts before a diverse public. We wanted to make our first symposium as broad as possible, so we invited unique bookmakers, letterpress bookmakers, offset editioned bookmakers, artists who have contributed works to fine press and artist's books, artists who have collaborated on artist's books, poets, writers who have written about the book as cultural object, writers who have collaborated on artist's books, art history scholars, literary scholars, press directors, book arts gallery directors, and book arts teachers. Some of the individual participants represent several of these areas of book arts activity in one person.

A primary link from the book arts to a wider artistic practice, as well as a link from the contemporary book arts period (late 1960s to the present) to earlier eras, is the tradition of artistic publishing activities included in the Fluxus movement. The great press stemming from, but by no means limited to, the Fluxus movement, is Something Else Press, founded and directed by Dick Higgins, which later permutated into Printed Editions. Something Else was a visual arts, literary, musical, and otherwise undefinable artistic enterprise which has provided a model for the book arts which few have equalled and none have surpassed. We asked Dick Higgins, therefore, to participate in *Art & Language: Re-Reading the Boundless Book.* The opening night of the symposium featured a performance by Alison Knowles, also a magnetic figure in the arts over the past thirty years, and one whose work includes the book arts yet extends beyond them. It is precisely this sense of a wide context in which the book is undefinable which we sought to convey. Knowles is a composer, performance artist, writer, and book artist. Her books include printed books of her multilayered writings and images (published, most recently, and magnificently, by Left Hand Books) as well as unique large-scale inhabitable book structures. Thus the first event of the symposium provided a historical basis (albeit recent history) for the book arts, a link of the book to live performance (the book off the page), and a sense of the limitless nature of the book arts.

The opening evening was followed by a day of talks by participants: Higgins, Knowles, Karen Wirth, Charles

Bernstein, Jo Anne Paschall, Linda Reinfeld, Toshi Ishihara, Brad Freeman, Johanna Drucker, Susan Bee, Byron Clercx, Colette Gaiter, Amos Paul Kennedy, Jr., Katherine Kuehn, and Steven Clay. These participants come from New York City, upstate New York, Minneapolis, St. Paul, Atlanta, Idaho, Chicago, Albuquerque, and Japan. Their topics range from the economics of small press publishing, to the use of historical source materials, to the social impact of teaching the book arts to children, to the hermeneutics of the book arts, to a consideration of one kind of Japanese literary game as book art. All in all, the symposium succeeded in providing any number of exciting departure points from which one might develop a deeper criticism of the book arts.

The talks in the symposium panels, which have now become the book you hold in your hands, were delivered, many of them, to the accompaniment of slide and video presentations. They have been edited here, for the most part, to include descriptions of the visual works presented, but so as not to absolutely require illustration. The idea was to encourage talk of the book arts as distinct from presentation of the book arts. Still, in some of these talks (most critically in Alison Knowles's, which inhabits the pages of this book as a kind of disembodied performance) you will notice the artists gesturing to "this picture," "that image," and other visual evidence of the work they are describing. We invite your imagination, for the most part, to realize the substance of the descriptive words. In only a few cases did we decide to present visual information which otherwise would have been entirely too obscure or unattainable.

The audience at the symposium included book artists and book enthusiasts in the Twin Cities and from around the nation. Their questions after talks and during receptions, readings, and exhibitions provided another aspect of this rich symposium which we can only tell you about. I mention it here to convey that the entire affair was one of high and serious informality, achieving the sense of a community in the early stages of defining its activities.

Minnesota Center for Book Arts offers these talks to you with the hope that you might find your own point of entry into the book arts and its criticism. We offer them with the hope that you might come to an understanding of the richness of activities in the field. The book is a familiar object, yet in the hands of artists it becomes transformative. We offer these talks as the informal presentations they were at the Minnesota Center for Book Arts studios, among a papermill, printing and bookbinding areas, and a gallery which was showing the concurrent exhibition, *Art & Language: Re-Reading the Boundless Book*. We hope you find in these talks some of the exciting possibilities for transformation of the book which provided an electric air during the days of the symposium, April 8 through April 10, 1994. We hope you agree with us that the future of the book, and of book arts theory and criticism, is truly boundless.

Hermeneutics and the Book Arts

Dick Higgins

Something that has always bothered me has been the unsuitability of the traditional ways of looking at works of art, for a lot of new art forms, particularly when they're still unfamiliar to us. This would include Fluxus-type pieces which I've been associated with, or concrete poetry or sound poetry or artist's books. And I've found that one way out of it is to try to apply hermeneutics, and specifically Gadamer's hermeneutics — Hans Jšrg Gadamer, for those who haven't run across his name. And so I wanted to present a hermeneutic model for you to keep in mind as you wander through trying to evaluate these pieces and to decide how they speak to you and what you are actually experiencing as you see them.

Hermeneutics has been a buzzword for some ten or fifteen years now, but it is also a seventeenth century word first used to describe methodologies of interpretation in biblical exegesis. In other words, a way to explain what the biblical phrase you might be looking at meant to the person who wrote it down, compared with how you read it today. And it focuses on this interaction between what is out there and what you have here as a conveyor of meaning. And so in hermeneutics we don't speak so much of an audience as of a receiver — the receiver of the message on all levels, on the semantic level, and on the gut level, the emotional level, the aesthetic level, all those kinds of things.

Gadamer has a metaphor, which he sticks to very closely in his writing about hermeneutics. And it's the metaphor of the horizon. Let's say, you as the receiver, come with your own horizon. You experience a work of art, which has its own horizon. While you're experiencing it, these horizons fuse. After you've experienced it, they separate again, but your horizon, now at least when you think about this piece, is a little bit changed. So that it matches this a little more closely. You have one horizon, another horizon, they fuse, and they separate, and have a little distortion. Now, if this fusion is profound so that you become involved in the thing, that should tell you that this work is somehow meaningful or challenging or something like that to you. When you separate out again, if you find that your horizon has been a little bit changed, or maybe a lot changed by the experience of what you've seen, then you can say to yourself, even if it's a work in a form that you know nothing about, that in one way or another it has had a powerful effect on you and you can begin to say that it's a meaningful work to you, on the emotional level, or on the intellectual level, however you want to put it.

I'm not going to get into Heidegger's "hermeneutic circles" and that kind of thing, because it's a very complex system. But Gadamer's metaphor I find extremely useful in explaining to myself why this artist's book that I'm looking at works, even though it doesn't seem to have any of the values that we associate with traditional art. That is, the text has been distorted, it's been changed, it's been modified. I may not even read every word of it, but the way that it's presented to me brings me into close contact with that artist's horizon and my own horizon is distorted and I remember it, feeling it in a strong way when I go away, if it works at its best.

Now, let's complicate the picture a little bit. This technique works for music, but in music, you have a double fusion, because you have, let's say, what the composer fused with his performer, or her performer, and then you have what you, as the receiver, perceive. Most of the time you have no way of going all the way back to the composer. But you have a sort of compound horizon that you do fuse with. So there are these other models. And the same would be true if the artist's book happens to be an artist's book which has a work of poetry in it.

This morning, Charles [Alexander] was talking about how the poem as it was written seems to be somehow a little separate from and even replaced by the poem as it is then typeset and presented. I think I'm quoting you correctly. And what has happened there, is that there's been a fusion of horizons between Charles and the typographer that he works with and the typographer has taken the original horizon and left it fused in a new form. And what we now see is this compound horizon, (what we receive,) and we look through the typographic one to an imagined version of Charles's poem, but we don't really know what Charles's poem looked like in its manuscript form. We know that some of the words were even changed when it was typeset, but we look through it to the implied horizon, and we have this compound horizon which is what we actually experience. And this experience is what I feel when I go to a good Fluxus performance, a good art performance, or any of the other ones where they really work and where I find myself at a loss to verbalize why they work if I don't use some methodology like this. So I offer this to you as a tool (not original with me) for approaching these kinds of things, in order that we be able to work towards a common critical vocabulary for evaluating these things over the years.

Embrace & Insight:
The Book Is a World

Steven Clay

I have some bits and pieces here that I'd like to share with you. This first quote is something I like to keep in mind whenever reading art history books, which I love to do, or attending symposiums on such matters, as this one. It comes from Jonathan Williams's quotebook, *In the Azure Over the Squalor*, and it's attributed to Barnett Newmann, who says, "Aesthetics is for artists, like ornithology is for the birds." Just something to keep in mind.

Nonetheless, what I'm going to speak about is a kind of felt-sensory experience. I do think that contexts are very important and useful, so I'm going to try to map out some of the concerns and resonances that I see present in the work I'm doing at Granary Books. The piece I want to read is roughly translated from the German artist Barbara Farner, whose work I've shown and published on two occasions.

The world is a book, the world is a mystery. Day and night, things send out messages which keep my curiosity ablaze. I constantly encounter limits I want to pass, and doors I want to push open. Defiance and a longing not to be shut up in this world any longer drive me continuously to investigate, examine, connect, distort, arrange, and collect. The book as idea for my activities. I am a collector and the book is the place where I keep my findings. Where I assort, order, combine and supplement them. In the book I play with my collection. I collect words, contexts, stories, facts, dates, speculations. I search the myths, read the poets, study the philosophers and travel to strange cultures. I pick up the numerous threads and I entwine and interlace them to weave a spider's web. My art is an encyclopedic art.

This next little bit is from Dick Higgins, from his preface to Joan Lyon's anthology *Artists' Books.*

Perhaps the hardest thing to do in connection with the artist's book is to find the right language for discussing it. Most of our criticism in art is based on the concept of a work with separable meaning, content and style — 'this is what it says' and 'here is how it says what it says.' But the language of normative criticism is not geared towards the discussion of an experience, which is the main focus of most artists' books.

Since 1982, Granary Books has gone through several transformations. Initially emerging as a distributor for fine press books, its present incarnation is as a fully self-supporting art gallery in Soho, where we make exhibitions of contemporary artists' books in the context of the greater milieu within which they exist. Which is to say that books are always shown along with the full range of an artist's work, be it paintings, drawings, video-installation, sculpture, whatever. We also host a range of extracurricular activities, poetry readings, lecture series, music series, forthcoming film series, and occasional performances. The reason for this is that the range of influences on artists who make books is large and diverse. For myself, as a gallerist and publisher, I can say that my most significant influences come not from the history of book publishing, but more from the general socio-cultural world of post-1945 art and music. First and foremost John Cage, but many others. For example, Carolee Sneeman, Stan Brakhage, Robert Duncan, Wallace Berman, Joseph Beuys — these are the people who I really look to, who I consider my heroes in some sense and who really incite a lot of what I try to encourage at Granary.

Everyone, or perhaps most of you in this room, will know Stephane Mallarmé's famous quote, "Everything in the world exists in order to end up as a book." Various traditions both archaic and current are geared toward their losing some of their specific identity. In part because of the gradual cross-fertilization which characterizes much of the art made during the past thirty years, it might be possible to isolate certain elements in a particular book. For example influences from the tradition of the *livre d'artiste* or the book object, the fine press

21

book, the cheap multiple, but for me this is not as compelling as the overall significance of each work as it is discovered in the hands and eyes of each reader. Hopefully one who is not overly concerned about arriving at some new strategy for classification.

On to a few books . . . As Johanna Drucker has so eloquently pointed out, behind all the books, there is the persistent legacy of the cultural icon of the book, as the law and the word, the diary, the secret place of interior life and the document of public record. The book is the Bible, the Koran, the Gospel, and the Psalms — the history of the creation and the prophecy of the apocalypse; but the book is also the checkbook, the phone book, the tiny black book of phone numbers, and the pocket edition carried on the subway, train, and plane. The book is the banal supermarket edition, the object laid away in the ark, the source of taboo, prohibition, the battle zone of censorship and transgression and expression and free speech, among other things, I'm sure. If I had to pick one, I would take the object laid away in the ark.

The operative metaphor that I have used in my publishing has come from Ezra Pound, "The book shd. be a ball of light in one's hands." The quality that I am most moved by, moved to nurture, exhibit and publish, is the intensely personal, and therefore universal and transformative. Or in the words of Jack Bernam in his essay "The Artist as Shaman," "It is precisely those artists involved in the most naked projections of their personalities, who will contribute most to society's comprehension of itself."

I'd like to describe some of the recent Granary publications. This is a picture of a granary, this at Chichen Itzá in Yucatan, Mexico, circa 800 AD. This is where they brought the corn and ground it up to make the food — it's a site of great nourishment. Chelaquile! This is a book entitled, *A Space for Breathing*. It was published in 1992. Chelaquile has said that

> There's an awareness of the body in my work process, and my installations become psychological extensions of the body. Concerns in my work are gestures of the body, gestures of the site, an architecture of emotion — the body as architecture.

Her work evokes a kind of epochal, psycho-sexual narrative spoken within our bodies, and within the architecture of the spaces our bodies inhabit. This book is made with color xerox transfers and original drawings in pencil, wax pigment, and gouache, in each of the 22 copies of the edition.

I'd like to insert a little production note here: one strand that weaves itself through many of the Granary publications is the use of original work by the artist in each of the works. There is no particular scheme or formula guiding the making of the books, other than the desire to let the art dictate its own form. I love drawing and collage, and have no particular desire to turn an artist into a printmaker, simply so that we can do a book. We generally, therefore try to find some aspect of the writer's work which can be mechanically reproduced, and then the lion's share of the work is done as a kind of meditation by the artist. We've used, so far, among the ten editions, letterpress, xerox, xerox-transfer, etching, and offset. Bindings are all designed by the alchemist/bookbinder Daniel Kelm, and produced by him and his staff at the Wide Awake Garage in Massachusetts. And they're specifically made to subtly bring the reader into the experience of the book, without drawing all the attention onto themselves. The typographical design is often made in collaboration with Philip Gallo of Hermetic press, whose 25 years as a concrete and visual poet aims at further elucidating the artists' vision. The protective boxes, which house the books, are nearly always purely functional and are all made by Jill Jevne.

Another recent book is entitled *Too Much Bliss*, by the artist Henrik Drescher. It's roughly modeled on the idea of the scrapbook or journal, it's subtitled "Scars, Tatoos, Cracks, Memories, Impressions, Flashbacks and Forgotten Instructions." The work is characterized by an unconditional passion, and, I believe, maps a total cosmology. In the words of one critic, "The book has the look of some manically encyclopedic new-age Sears-and-Roebuck mail order catalog of all the elements that ever existed in the course of organic history and human memory." The pages are letterpress printed from the artists' drawings and then they have been hand-treated with the paint, collage, and more drawing, in an edition of 41.

Scrutiny in the Great Round, by another New York Artist named Tennessee Rice Dixon, is a collage book, and it draws from a range of sources from seventeenth century alchemical engravings to twentieth century high school science textbook illustrations. The book traces a transformative lifeline from before conception to after birth, invoking images of intimacy, courtship, conception, birth, sexuality, fertility, agriculture, nutrition, food. It's an interpretation of history and a myth of individual redemption. The edition of 22 was made with xerox, painting, drawing, and collage.

Because of their legacy, intimate scale, and everyday presence, I believe that books have the ability to embrace and incite a total experience. This is what I find most interesting, most telling about artists' books, and what I've strived to achieve and convey in the books that I have published. I have two more quotes here. This one is from Joseph Beuys,

> The development of art as everybody instinctively knows, is one of the most important things in the world because it reflects the fact that secret things are condensed, especially in human beings. So the movement of art in words is a kind of approach to this threshold.

And I'm going to close with another bit of Barbara Farner's statement on her work, which I think applies to a lot of our work.

> Mostly I speak in pictures. My thoughts and my imagination primarily express themselves in pictures. I find a language of pictures to be the most wonderful and greatest art. I can be

captivated by a speech text, by a piece of music, but the thunderbolt that flashes through my body into my soul and which sends the tears to my eyes always comes from a picture. I use the metaphor, the world is like a book, literally, pictorially. To imitate and record the diversity and the abundant canon of forms in the world I need the largest field of expression available. I use the type, the abstract, the design, the image, the formula. There exists a vast power to combine these means of expression. What one should take note of when looking at, and into, my books, is that the book is not the text-carrier: the typography is not the pages' adornment; the pictures are not the writings' illustration; the book is a manifold, living being. The book is a world.

A Critical Metalanguage for the Book as an Artform

Johanna Drucker

It seemed to me that my task for this symposium was to think about what a book could be, in critical terms. So I put my mind to work, and unfortunately it turned out to be fairly prosaic. I came up with all kinds of categories of structure — things like openings, gutters, dimensions, layout. Then I thought, I think I need to make this more interesting. It's got to be critical, conceptual, ideological —

But then I responded with an instinctive protest — No! No! No! What I really want to think about is secrecy, intimacy, privacy — all those things that led me to the Book in the first place. And so, this dialogue emerged between a personal, private voice and a critical, theoretical voice.

I began to be interested in books as a child because I wanted to write *all of the time,* and so wore a notebook around my neck, with a pen attached, in order to be inscribing the world as response — and that was sometime before age ten, I know. I remember because of the shape of my body, and the way the book hung down. I was still prepubescent, exempt from self-consciousness about the dangling items —

But let's go back to this problem of critical terms: what is the nature of openings? What is the relation of pages to each other across the gutter, the dialogic interplay of face to face, a kind of conversation, confrontation if one wishes, or companionship in space, the parallel condition, feeling ordered by the sequence, but not needing to be.

And then, switching back to my private passions: The writing was to be hidden. I made it very, very small, as if it were an interior trace, not readable or available to any other eye but made for the sake of the belief in the act.

And the critical voice answered: What structures are specific to the book, then? There is after all that statement that a book is a "sequence of spaces" suggested by Ulisses Carion. But then there are also gutters, gutters of which I was barely aware until Brad Freeman showed me Clifton Meador's work and the ways it insisted in the creeping intrusion, subliminal play, of elements creeping into the pages from that dark space which is the spine. Only a binding which does not open itself, flat, doesn't make itself available, isn't honest and forthright, can support such mysterious gutters, such areas of fertile activity, breeding its furtive forms in the dark enclosure.

Then the private voice: A book has to be closed, tight, to preserve its power. The potency of spells, formulae, maintained by their inaccessibility. We know, we know, Pandora's box was a book of knowledge hastily opened and long lost.

Critical: Now the dimensions of the book's form also

cause a certain tension, stretching the eye to the longest horizon of a line, a page, a paragraph condensed or slung out long and low. Or it may be harmonious, these tensions of dimension, in keeping with some guarantee of relations — a golden mean, a perfect trine, a strictly ruled and regulated space of margins text and tribulations. There can be the weight of pages sinking to the floor with all their pretense or their difficulties — height to width, side to side, arm to arm, a veritable exercise of visual aerobics.

The personal voice: I read her like a book. Ah yes, the metaphors of book-ness — open, available, clear and accessible. Organized, self-evident, presenting as a map of readability as if a character would or could ever be so bold, so to the point and on the surface. Still, the metaphor insists upon the possibility.

And critical again: Sometimes it seems like layout and format are wrestling companions interlocking until one is felled, held, and pronounced upon. There is the machismo of type and language getting a grip on the mack truck of the image, or going it alone, into a different line of tropes — the ruly and the irregular, the ungovernable and the meek, the lines which lay down with the lion and those which stroll all over the landscape with the lamb. There are the elements of disorderly conduct or organizational expertise, offering up the substance of the work according to their own terms of decorum — or endearment.

Personal: They threw the book at him. And so they should have, except for what that meant to the ancient binding and the fragile pages — still, the whole exhaustive inventory of the Law, what a formidable weight, one sees, a disproportion between the size of the projectile and the size of its intended target so that one or the other is demeaned, humiliated, and subject.

Critical: Sequence, in fact, is the great structural instrument of the book — its method, its madness, its order, its progression — writhing into a serpentine trail of mixed messages and interlocking narratives, the browsing method of the tabloid, the reliable order of the alphabetic sequence, the dependable linearity of normative prose, the irrepressible experience of images forging their connections through the fact of following, one after another, in the fixed determination of a regulated encounter. We lift off, from the flat platform of the program, into the flight of an interactive fancy — coming and going from the finitude of pages in the places and our own unpredictable encounter. Their order against our whim, their fixity against our interference, their sense against our disregard for it.

Personal: The book of the world, the word, the book of nature, the book of knowledge, the book of light and the books which had to be okayed by the librarian before they could be taken out. I chose mine for the thinness of paper, the smallness of type, and number of pages. I wanted commitment from a book, a sense that if we got involved, it would last. A long time.

Critical: Movement and timing, the flicker of papers, colors, textures, elements. Janet Zweig's extremely receptive book, turning the radar dish around and around in itself, as if that remote interior could be the site for sore messages or prying eyes. Suppleness and stiffness, the resistance and cooperation of materials. The sensual theater of the Iliazd books, lifting their thin veils one after another before the heavy curtain of the stiff interior. Now all of that is available as simulations — paper textures printed on coated stock in imitation of the handmade, hard to handle, fetishized original.

Personal: They'll make a book from that movie, just you wait! The absurdity of text following on media, becoming necessary only to be owned and provide the private experience of the public spectacle.

Critical: From the structural to the conceptual — a leap from the observation of form as specific to the medium to the associative play of form as idea: the metaphysics of the book, its full range of roles from initiation and knowledge to perfidy and deceit. The tiny diary revealing all, the elephant folio displaying its riches and wares, the fine fine insights of the well-wrought manual, explaining itself without difficulty to the real material of some other world. Reference and reverence, physics and dynamics, blindness and the raw face of insight staring back from the pages and into the backlit screen of the mind. The trials and tribulations of sanctity, betrayal, violation, and the mutilated record all bound into the affective legacy of the Book not merely as Object — as far as I am concerned, any book with its pages glued shut is not engaged in a dialogue — but Book as Topic as Subject as Prospect and Charge.

In the end, the voices synthesize their response: And finally, not least, the endlessly mutating status of the book as a

commodity which identifies itself with confusion these days —
the portable companion, the fetishized original, the almost a
portfolio, the tale of the literal, the visual, the virtual — all
vying for a place in the marketplace of saleable, tradeable,
identifiable items for consumption, sale, and resale. The book
is value — blue book — in itself and for others — the guest
book the social register the family album the scrapbook the
black book — its social and cultural functions weaving in and
out of its functional and ideational identity. What is the book
to be, now, in the interspace of hyperelectronic nodes? A nexus
of events? A momentary intersection of concerns? An
immaterial form of non-record of what might have been ideas
or events? Or a new form of that Mallarmean mutation, that
final, realized Book which is the full equivalent of both the
world and the self, the total spiritual symbol of knowledge as
complete, replete, and yet, satisfyingly bounded into itself. A
whole. Or is it instead to be an endless fragmentation, in
which we all, each, have our part to play in writing, scribing,
projecting, painting ourselves as a place in the constellation of
a synaesthetic newspeak.

The book remains. That, I think, has been the cause of
my attachment to it. The fact of its independent life, its
capacity to go out from the shop, the house, the office, and live
on its own. As Todd Walker says, the joy of it all is that you
can find it again, years later, on a shelf, and it still works —
without batteries, lights, or electricity, it makes itself available
again, as a new experience, a new encounter.

The Economics of the Small Press: Poetry Publishing

Charles Bernstein

Today we have heard many presentations about B-O-O-K technology, a technology that reinvents itself as the cutting edge of alphabetic hyperspace. We've seen its remarkable versatility, its rugged state-of-the-art packaging, its astounding portability, its unequaled unit cost, the remarkable ease of its user interface — almost no training costs or tutorials needed to access its materials. And also today we've seen the unbelievably high level of graphic resolution allowed by B-O-O-K technology, without the need for GIF and other sophisticated computer decoding programs and devices.

But, I want now to turn to a topic that is somewhat different from the other aspects of book arts that have been discussed today — the relation of books and book production and book arts to poetry publications. And I want to mention the great work of Dick Higgins and Something Else Press as being an inspiration for this particular area of poetry publishing. It is a pleasure to be on the panel with Dick.

Poetry book and poetry magazine publishing rarely enters into the more radical and self-conscious domain of the book arts since there is a general preference to make books that do not call extra attention to their material and conceptual dimensions. But, nonetheless, poetry publishing is an especially important area for writers' direct involvement in the production of books.

I am conscious that I am giving this talk in Minneapolis, which is such an important center for the small press. Consortium, one of the most important poetry and book distributors in the United States, is located here. Coffee House Press is located here. Chax Press, and its editor, Charles Alexander, have recently moved here. I am thinking also of Gary Sullivan and Marta Deike, who have brought their fabulous *Stifled Yawn* to the Twin Cities, only to let it die a humorous death here; but also the rebirth as Detour Press, their new press, and I think also, for my purposes, *e.g.,* which they've taken over, which is a typical micropress, the sort of operation which I think is the very heart of poetry production in the United States.

The past thirty years have been a time of enormous growth of small press publishers. According to Loss Pequeno Glazier, statistics in *Small Press: An Annotated Guide*, the number of magazines listed in Len Fulton's *International Directory of Little Magazines and Small Presses* has gone from 250 mostly poetry magazines in 1965, to 700 in 1966, to 2,000 magazines in 140 categories in 1976, to 4,800 magazines in 1990, of which about 40% were literary. The importance of the small press for poetry is not restricted to any aesthetic or indeed to any segment of poets. According to a recent study by Mary Briggs, the independent, noncommercial presses are a major source of exposure for all poets — young and old, prize-winning or not.

The staple of the independent literary press is the single-author poetry collection. Douglas Messerli, publisher of Sun & Moon Press, a high-end small press comparable to Black Sparrow, New Directions, and Dalkey Archive, provided me with some representative publication information for a 100-page poetry collection:

Print runs at Sun & Moon go from 1,000 to 2,000, depending, of course, on likely sales. Messerli notes that print runs of less than 1,000 drive the unit costs up too high and he encourages all literary presses to print a minimum of 1,000 copies if at all possible.

Sun & Moon titles are well-produced, perfect bound, and offset with full color covers. The printing bill for this runs from $2,600 to $4,000 as you go from 1,000 to 2,000 copies. Messerli estimates the cost of editing a 100-page poetry book at $300: this covers all the work between the press receiving the manuscript and sending it to a designer (including any copyediting and proofreading that may be necessary, as well as preparation of front and back matter and cover copy). Typesetting is already a rarity for presses like Sun & Moon, with authors expected to provide computer disks wherever possible. Formatting these disks can cost anywhere from $300 to $1,000, one of those variable labor costs typical of small press operations. The book designer will charge about $500. The cover will cost an additional $100 for photographic reproduction and permission fees for both. Publicity costs must also be accounted for, even if, as with Sun & Moon, no advertising is involved. Messerli estimates publicity costs at $1,500, which covers the cost of something like 100 free copies distributed to reviewers, postage and packing, mailing a catalog pages, etc. The total cash outlay here, then, for 2,000 copies is around $6,800. (For the sake of this discussion, overhead costs — rent, salary, office space, phones — are not included. Such costs typically are estimated at about 30% more than the cost of production.)

If all goes well, Sun & Moon will sell out of its print run in two years. Let's say Sun & Moon prints 2,000 copies of the book and charges $10 retail. Let's also say that all of the books were sold. That makes a gross of $20,000. Subtract from this a 50% wholesale discount (that is, most bookstores will pay $5 for the book) and that leaves $10,000. Subtract from this the 24% that Sun & Moon's distributor takes (and remember that most small presses are too small to secure a distributor with a professional sales force, like Consortium). That leaves $7,600. Now, last, but not to be totally forgotten, especially since I am a Sun & Moon author, the poet's royalty; typically, no advance would be paid and the author would receive 10% of the last figure, or $760. That leaves $6,840 returned to the publisher on a cash cost of about $7,000.

As James Sherry noted in $L=A=N=G=U=A=G=E$ years ago; a piece of paper with nothing on it has a definite economic value — if you print a poem on it, this value is lost. We have here a vivid example of what George Bataille has called general economy, an economy of loss rather than accumulation. Poetry is a negative — or let's say poetic — economy.

But of course I've stacked the decks a bit. Many small presses will eat a number of the costs I've listed. Copyediting, proofreading, and design costs may be absorbed in the overhead if they are done by the editor-cum-publisher, proofreader, publicity department, and shipper. Formatting and production are commonly done on in-house computers. But these costs cannot be absorbed away — 600 dpi laser printers and late-night proofreading can cause some serious malabsorption problems, for which your gastroenterologist has no cure. Then again, if a book generates enough of an audience to require reprinting, modest profits are possible, allowing the publication of other, possibly less popular, works.

The situation for independent literary magazines is quite similar, and I could give you similar statistics for that. But of course many small presses and magazines produce more modest publications than Sun & Moon. Indeed, the heart of the small press movement is the supercheap magazine or chapbook, allowing just about anyone to be a publisher or editor. In this world, marketplace values are truly turned upside down, since many readers of small press poetry feel the more modest the production, the greater the integrity of the content. There is no question that many of the best poetry magazines of the postwar period have been produced by the cheapest available means. In the 1950s the mimeo revolution showed up the stuffy pretensions of the established, letterpress literary quarterlies, not only with their greater literary imagination, but also with innovative designs and graphics. In 1965, 23% of literary presses were mimeo, 31% offset, 46% letterpress, according to Fulton's Directory. By 1973, offset had jumped to 69%, with letterpress at 18%, and mimeo only 13%. As Loss Glazier notes, the mimeo in "the mimeo revolution" is more a metaphor for inexpensive means of reproduction than a commitment to any one technology. Indeed, poetry's use of technology has often had a wryly aversive quality. For example, as offset began to dominate the printing industry in the early 1970s, letterpresses became very cheap to acquire and innovative letterpress printers, such as some of the people here, could produce books with little other cash expense than paper costs and mailing, given the editor's willingness to spend hundreds of hours to handset every letter and often hand-feed each page.

In the metaphoric sense, the mimeo revolution is very much alive in the 1990s with some of the very best poetry magazines today consisting of little more than a staple or two holding together from 16 to 60 sheets of paper xeroxed in editions of 50 or 100 or 150. To a lesser extent, this is also true of book publishing. I think that it is useful to raise this point in the context of the very many beautiful productions that are the primary focus of this gathering in order to show you how persistent and vital this kind of *low-end* publishing is.

The social and aesthetic meaning of these low-end

forms should not be underestimated. Books are never neutral mediums delivering up linguistic content, but rather contribute to the meaning and experience of the work. The mimeo revolution and its contemporary extensions often signify an opposition to the glossier, conventional formats of the more established literary magazines. The 60's mimeo magazines and books suggested, by their form, a seriousness, indeed an authenticity. This tactic of turning an economic necessity into an asset is part of the overall poetics that includes the style of writing as well as the book format. I want to just give you two examples designed by Susan Bee, my long-time collaborator, of what I mean by very cheap low-end forms having an aesthetic and social meaning in terms of the poetry readership in general. *L=A=N=G=U=A=G=E*, which I edited with Bruce Andrews from 1978 to 1981 went through thousands of copies in this form — typed on legal-size pages on our electric typewriter, sprayed so that the type wouldn't smear and then cut and pasted. Almost no gutters, almost no margins, as many people noted. No white space at all. And what this signifies — I'm trying to talk about ways you can 'read' design — is that we felt that there was an enormous absence of discussion about poetry and poetics at this time and what we wanted to do was to focus attention on this discussion as continuing and direct. This visual design seemed to suggest that. There were other choices as well: we always had the authors' names at the end of their articles and there's no table of contents so that each issue reads as a continuous discussion or dialogue, anticipating in some ways aspects of e-mail listserves of the present, but, of course, much more curated. My other example is Susan's design for *M/E/A/N/I/N/G*, shocking within the context of the visual art world — no graphics, no pictures, just pure text, again, slightly more white space but not that much, no pictures on the cover. *M/E/A/N/I/N/G*'s straightforward design reflects its social meaning to present mostly artists writing on art outside of the context of the commercial art world, as represented by glossy art magazines and books with color repros and high cover prices.

Poetry publishers and writers typically use standard and received forms of style as much as typography, of stanza format as well as of book designs to signify the "literary" nature of the work, (e.g., the use of initial caps, or the many cliches of "elevated" quality that mark the design of letterpress reprints of Shakespeare's sonnets and so on). Nothing should call attention, in that sense, to the material or semantic nature of the typography or the book design or the style, except as a mark of elegance or sumptuousness in some letterpress verse editions. The "disappearance" or transparency of typography, paper, texture, book design and the like (to borrow Ron Silliman's concept) is comparable to the stylistic ideal that a good sentence should not call attention to itself. In the regime of conventional literature neither the writing style *nor* the design should call attention to itself! In contrast, what I call antiabsorptive works may use all of these features in their resistance to exactly this textual and design transparency. To approach a *book* of poetry in this way not as a "text", a pure linguistic event, but as a *work* is to go against the prevalent critical paradigms of our time, where the meaning of verbal language is imagined to be independent if (that is to say, only arbitrarily connected to) the sound of words as well as independent of the visual representation of words. In this view, the phonotext and the visual representation are both viewed as arbitrary, whereas I'm insisting that the acoustic and visual dimensions of verbal language are semantic elements of the poetic work. There is no poem apart from its material dimension, in typography or in a performance. On this question, let me call your attention to the new book by one of this conference's participants. In *The Visible Word*, (University of Chicago, 1994) Johanna Drucker makes clear how crucial the visual representation of language is to meaning.

Poetry is a medium that activates the sonic and the visual, as well as the syntactic and paratactic, dimensions of language. That is, we can understand the book *as* our medium, much as the canvas is the medium for the painter: the physical space in which the poem is set. We can regard this space as a neutral repository for a text that exists as a verbal autonomy, or we can acknowledge the idealization of that assumption, recognize that it is not the *same* poem published in a different physical setting. (Computers, I would say, constitute a different medium from books. One might speak of a CD-ROM version of a poem as a transcription, as in a piano transcription of an orchestral work.) The book will persist because it is a distinct medium. Nonetheless, as we have repeatedly seen, the dominant technology will marginalize other technologies.

41

Drucker's new book shows the value of close readings of the visual aspects of a poetic work as a necessary supplement to thematic, contextual, structural, and acoustic readings. Basic design choices for poetry books do not have to foster either neutrality or fine press "elevation" through their choice of invisibility or lavishness, in both cases harmonizing the various design elements. Design elements can be used at cross purposes to create a collage or montage of *clashing* elements, chordal designs. That is to say, the elements used chordally create a synthesis that is very invisible. Design in this sense is not extra-linguistic, not extra-semantic, but contributes to the total meaning complex that is the book.

Let me end by mentioning some very elementary design features that poets can use proactively, rather than reactively, in creating their work. First, the size of the book, for which we need only recall the long format of Mallarme's *A Throw of the Dice Will Never Abolish Chance*. Second, typography; for example, using multiple clashing types. I would compare this to a performance of a poem that uses different voices to indicate different tones and different styles. Though I recognize that type does not have to be uniform, most typesetters, most poets value the uniformity and unobtrusiveness of typography. Leading is an even more recessive design element in most books of poetry than choice of font. Yet for one, there is a big difference between 11 on 13, 11 on 15, and 11 on 22. There's no such thing as a natural length between one line and the next; mostly each generation of type designers decides on a set of standard specifications. If you look at the history of books you see that, of course, leading has been done in many different ways. Third, visual design decisions may inform the line size or line breaks. Line lengths should not be simply looked at as by-products of syllable and word counts, syntactic/phrasal choices, or sound cues (pauses).

The length of the line is also a visual cue. That is, lines are as much a visual break as a notation of syntactic or temporal elements in the phonotext. You could argue here that William Carlos Williams' famous step lines or Charles Olson's famous breath lines are actually visual design elements whose primary innovation is in terms of page layout. The page, then, is the fourth visual element. So that, again, the horizontal flush left could also be done flush right, or flush center; and you have poems scored by page, as in Olson's or Susan Howe's "field" compositions. So that rather than stanzas we might think about lines and groupings of lines; line lengths, (very short individual-word lines, unequal line lengths).

A fifth element is punctuation. A minimalist approach to punctuation is to have a text be as unmarked as possible; another approach is to use standard forms, such as capital letters at the beginning of sentences and periods at the end. A minimalist might set everything in lower case, with no periods, no commas. At the other extreme, how about punctuating in the middle of words, using semicolons and other punctuational devices to disrupt or materialize the page. I think of Stein, especially, and some of her great pages.

Finally, there is paper — type and color of paper. (Though I must say, I have a hard time with that one, but, who knows, I do have some books by some people printed on purple and pink and yellow.) Printing method, of course. Images are one element within this total mix and that's the visual element that has mostly been discussed here. I am simply remembering that type is a visual element, an image element itself. Nor do I want to neglect binding. I think for example, of Robert Grenier's great work *Sentences*, 500 cards stacked together in a Chinese box which can be read in any order, usually multiple orders. Grenier's box reminds us that the concept of hypertext is inherent within writing and alphabet technology, that writing and alphabet technology is only 4,000 years old and is still a revolutionary new form that is wildly under-accessed in our society. Insofar as we get excited about newer means of accessing texts, that's great; but the alphabet itself and the visual representation of language that it makes available is still something which leaves an enormous area to be explored.

Social Book Building

Amos Paul Kennedy, Jr.

I would like to begin my talk by taking a survey that I take wherever I speak. It's a participation. Have any of you either read or produced a book about the victims of AIDS? — Would you raise your hands? An artist's book, fine print book about AIDS . . . o.k. they're out there. Now, have any of you read or produced a book about the genocide that is occurring in America of children under age fourteen? Two people. I believe that there is a conspiracy in America at present. A conspiracy to kill poor children. In 1992, 254 children under the age of *one year* were murdered in the *great* United States of America. In Chicago, in 1991, 60 children under the age of fourteen were murdered; in 1993, 62 under fourteen were murdered.

I was struck by this fact in 1992 when an article appeared in the Chicago Tribune. What really got me was that if 62 poets had been murdered there would be volumes of memorial poetry, there would be readings, libraries would have ceremonies. If 62 musicians were murdered symphonies would write requiems for them, the Orchestra Hall would probably shut down for a night. If 62 artists were murdered, the School of the Art Institute would probably close up for a day to honor them, or be draped in black. Sixty-two children were murdered and there wasn't a *whisper* from the art community or from any community at all. Why is it that 62 lives can be taken and there is no reaction from the art community?

I continue to look for reasons. This year, Caren Heft and I have established a program called *Children Don't Count*. We are attempting to get at least one printer in each state to do a book dedicated to the children who were murdered — children who were shot, beaten to death, lynched, or stabbed. If we can get a printer from each state to memorialize the children from that state it will be the first time volumes of this nature have ever been done for these victims. And children are truly victims.

Why I Am a Social Printer?

Last week I was rereading an essay by Langston Hughes entitled "My Adventures as a Social Poet." He starts by saying,

> Poets who write mostly about love, roses and moonlight, sunsets and snow, must lead a very quiet life. Seldom, I imagine, does their poetry get them into difficulties. Beauty and lyricism are really related to another world, to ivory towers, and to your head in the clouds, feet floating off the earth. Unfortunately, having been born poor — and also colored —

in Missouri, I was stuck in the mud from the beginning. Try as I might to float off into the clouds, poverty and Jim Crow would grab me by the heels, and right back on earth I would land.

I am a SOCIAL PRINTER! Whatever I print — because my work is dedicated to the documentation of Negro culture — whatever I print is political. When I print the love poems of Georgia Douglas Johnson, or the love poems of Paul Laurence Dunbar, because these are Black poets, Black authors, there is a political side to the volume. The poems would never be printed as love poems by European fine press printers.

How many of you have seen a fine print book, an artist's book, where the subject matter is about Black people or the author is a black person? Of all the books that are done each year, what is it? One percent? Two percent? At one time I was really bitter about this, but then I thought about it and I said well, how many books are done about Native Americans? How many are done about Japanese-Americans? Chinese-Americans? How many books do book artists make about their own culture? Are they printing the work of white male poets because that is what sells, or because that's what is supposed to be popular? I have taken the stance that whatever I do will be done to promote my people. And I was told by the Dean of Letterpress in Chicago, Bruce Beck, that this is a novel approach because most people he knows who have a press do not have a mission statement as radical as mine. I said, "Well, it goes with my character."

The Book As A Political Tool

Through my mis-education I have arrived at the conclusion that the book is a political tool. We can look at the book and the history of the book. Up until Gutenberg's printing press, books were made in monasteries and were kept by the church, which was a real power in government. In the Middle Ages, the average citizen could not read, so a book was a mystical thing that the clergy held, opened up and read from. There were symbols in it and they, the clergy, read from the book, but the average person could not, so the book conveyed the power of the church. When you look at the *Book of Kells,* the size and the illumination, the design conveyed the power of the church to the peasants.

After Gutenberg, books became more plentiful, but they became plentiful for the merchant class, for the bourgeois, and for the townspeople. During the Renaissance it was quite common for a Renaissance "yuppie" to have a nice library, even if he didn't read the books. It was a status symbol. "Here are the books that I have and these are the writers and printers." It wasn't until, I guess, about the mid-nineteenth century that books really became commonplace because of the industrial revolution. Two things, I believe, occurred. First, in order to run a machine, a better trained work force was needed. So, workers had to have some sort of education. Second, printing equipment became more efficient, so more things could be printed. From about 1850 onward, books became plentiful and began to invade every man's home. It wasn't until the 1910s and 1920s that the book really invaded the home. There was also, at this time, a rush of what I call self-help books, self-improvement books. If you lived in a city, but weren't able to go to the colleges, you were able to get the self-improvement books and read Plato, Socrates and become enlightened.

So all along the book has been a political tool used to manipulate people, and it continues to be. I think it will always be, because it is easier to manipulate people and keep them down if they are uneducated. The last thing that this country wants, despite everything the politicians say, is an educated populace, because if any of you have ever dealt with educated people you know they don't get along. Educated people will argue all the time to get their point across. So, when the politicians say we want better education, that's a ruse. What they want is to train people for positions. No one ever says that they want to educate people so that they can become better human beings. Rather, we want to train kids so they can get jobs when they get out of school. In other words, we need a resource for our workplace — we need to have little robots to man positions in industry.

The Book Under Attack

At the present time, I see the book being attacked on two fronts. The first front is general illiteracy, that is, people don't read as much as they once did, despite the fact that more books are being printed. I think the few people who read are reading more, but more people are not reading. The other threat is automation, the great wonder called the computer, which will solve all of our problems. If everyone could just get one on their desk and enter into the super highway . . . I have some reservations about what automation will do. I sincerely believe that despite all of the hoopla that's going on right now about automation, Internet and the information highway, that within my son's lifetime, text based automation will become obsolete. I believe the computer will become voice activated and voice simulation will get better, so instead of someone sitting down and reading a text, they'll say, "read it to me." The screen will become obsolete, unless it is used as a TV set to watch movies or images of the "spoken words". This is interesting because before the advent of the book, all information was transmitted verbally, by word of mouth. "What my father told me, I told my sons and my sons told their sons." It will be interesting to see what happens as the technologies become more sophisticated.

Illiteracy can be conquered if we *want* to conquer it. Because of the importance of the book in society right now, all children should be able to read. All people, citizens of this country, should be able to read. A large portion of the country can't read, there are numbers of children in school who will never be able to read despite the fact that they will have a high school diploma. We must address this *shame*. I have a son who just turned eight. When he was seven, he began to read out loud. If you have children you know that when they have mastered the art of reading they become very proud. "Daddy, I want to read this to you because I can read," and there is a gleam in his eye. It is almost as if it is the first time that children make a connection, and I call it a "golden connection" which occurs when you are working on something and suddenly you understand it all. This power comes to you through knowledge. I think when a child can read out loud and understand what she is reading, that this is the first time they make this connection with learning, with becoming educated, with having knowledge. The love of knowledge is developed at this point. If we can take this time in a child's life, normally between the ages of seven and eight, and couple it with book building it will teach children that they can take this complicated object called a book and make one. It is empowering. You may not save every child, but if you save one, that's one who would have been lost. I MUST teach book building as a part of literacy training.

Slavery, the institution of slavery and the racist policies that existed in America before 1865 did not appear overnight. It took 20 to 30 years for the laws and social attitudes of racism to develop. The process of social engineering at its best. One of the first things denied to Africans was the right to read. It was a crime to teach Africans to read. After emancipation, the first thing blacks did was to read openly or learn to read. Schools were established all over the South to teach the freed slaves how to read. Reading is a very powerful thing. It is an activity that, because we can do it, we may take for granted. Suppose you couldn't read and you saw somebody with a sheet of paper with symbols on it that they could decipher. Automatically the person with the power to decipher the

51

symbols becomes magical, mystical and is in a different class from you. I believe reading has a greater appeal to people than writing. If forced to choose, most people would rather be able to read than write, although we always think of the two of them together. Reading, the power of reading, is something we have to instill in children. We have to encourage reading in our school systems as much as possible. When you start to read, however, you start to become educated and education runs contrary to the forces of business. An educated man will find it difficult to sit at a desk for eight hours pushing paper that has no importance whatsoever. An educated man might find it difficult to say, "Well, I'm here because of the money. I have no personal satisfaction, but I'm getting a paycheck and that's the important thing." An educated man will ask questions. I'm quite sure that some of you have questioned the validity of your jobs and that if it wasn't for the mortgage you probably wouldn't be there. Nevertheless, we have to bring book building to children to encourage knowledge, the power of knowledge, for literacy.

The Wustum VIP Book Project

Last summer I had the opportunity to work in Racine, Wisconsin for a week with ten children who had been identified as being "at risk" for either joining gangs or doing drugs. The week before I got there, each child wrote a short essay about his or her favorite things. The week I was there we built a book. We started on Monday, making paper. Tuesday and Wednesday the children printed the text on a small portable press. I set the type at Caren Heft's studio on Monday and Tuesday nights. Thursday, they made illustrations for the books with cardboard prints. Finally, on Friday, the children bound the books. To celebrate the project, we took copies of the book to the Racine Public Library and the children presented them to the Children's Librarian. It was very rewarding to see these children who, *according to society*, are "at- risk" children who have low self-esteem, experience the joy of making a book of their own. They could go home to their families and say "This is what I have made, this is MY book." I told them that whatever might happen to the book they had at home, there will always be one at the library. "When you are 20 or 25 years old and have your own children you can say, 'Come on I want to show you the book I made,' and it will be there." They felt good about it. So kids like to build books, all kids; Black kids, White kids, rich kids, poor kids.

Please Start Your Own Project

What we need to do is get out there in the community and have them start building books. This is part of the mission of my press; at least once a year, I identify a needy group and go out and build books with them. It is difficult to do. The public schools have a bureaucracy which is designed to minimize the amount of education the children experience. Private schools have cliques. If you're not in the clique, you can't get in. You may knock on many doors that will not open, but you should continue to knock because if you can get one

53

child, if you can experience the excitement of one child building a book, only a few things are as wonderful. You know when you pull a proof that really looks good, you get a sort of high. When you have a child who says, "This is my book," and he clings to it, it's the same feeling. As a book artist I CANNOT, I WILL NOT sit in an ivory tower and discuss the merits of one typeface over another. I am a social book builder. I probably am not really a book artist, I am a craftsperson. I build books the old fashioned way, one page at a time. I want to pass this on, if not to my sons, to my sons' generation because if we do not, we will lose a whole generation of children. When they are lost, they are going to be like the hordes at the gates of Rome — they won't care what they destroy, they will destroy for the sake of destruction. If we hold these things sacred, if we treasure them, then we must share them. We must share our love for this thing called a book, with not just a select number of people, but all people. I would like for each of you to consider yourself a social printer. You may say, well, I don't want to get up in the street and raise a flag, I don't want to march down to city hall and voice my opinion to the school board. There are other things you can do.

Recently I heard on the radio a commentary by THAT *great white-appointed leader of African-Americans.* He said that he was walking down a street in Washington, D.C. and he got scared because he heard footsteps behind him. He turned around and saw that it was a White man following him and he was relieved. What I heard him say was that he is scared of little Black boys walking up behind him. I don't blame him; I'd be scared of anyone walking up behind me. There are places in America where Black people are uncomfortable walking down their streets and there are Black people on these streets, both the scared and the intimidators. My people are losing hope.

You will find that trends in the Black community are like the canaries in the nineteenth century mines, an early warning system for American society. About twenty years ago the public policy makers were ranting and raving about unwed mothers in the Black community. Now unwed mothers are found in every segment of American society. Twenty years ago society was ranting and raving about drugs in the Black community. Now drugs are common in all segments of society. If the loss of hope is confronting the Black community today, let it be an early warning to the rest of America. Loss of hope for all of us is around the corner.

When you build your books, remember that there is a public out there much larger than the 5,622 collectors, book artists and public libraries in America. Address your books to the rest of the community.

Design Elements in *Nude Formalism* and *Fool's Gold*

Susan Bee

Charles Bernstein and I have worked on several books collaboratively as well as many books separately. Today I'll be focusing on two of the books we've worked on together — *The Nude Formalism* from 1989 and *Fool's Gold*, which we worked on in 1990 and which was published in 1991. I won't be discussing *The Occurrence of Tune,* another collaboration from 1981, which involved altered photographs by me with a full-length poem by Charles.

The Nude Formalism was created as part of a series of 20-page offset books published by Sun & Moon Press in Los Angeles, which is mostly a poetry and fiction press. The book is very small — 5 by 7½ inches. In it I've set a series of Charles's individual poems in different type styles including advertising display fonts, text fonts, decorative fonts, and various types of ornamental borders, mostly clip art. This book was not done by computer. This was pre-computer. It was pasted up by hand. The idea of the book was to frame

Gosh

When fled I found my love defamed in clang
Of riotous bed she came, along the flues
I harbored there, scarce chance upon harangue
By labors grant the fig of latched amuse
She quakes and bless her soul would harsh realize
That none our maps could burn aboard her ship
And floral flung to fit parts cleared eyes
Left like that elder hap that splits a chip
When dull's the deed wherewith else back I on
Forewent all trial asleep her carousel
Thread in torching tease tuned basilican
Drifting after still much breath-crested scrawl
Hence going beads each languorous thronement
When all I gown errs come again cement

Fragments from the Seventeenth Manifesto of Nude Formalism

by Hermes Hermeneutic

Away with the study of flotation!

Articulation is more than an manner of gritting the pendulum!

Down with all authentic formulations of these theses! Down with Adolescent Sublime! Down with Abstract Confessionalism! Down with Empathic Symbolism! Down with Symbolic Empathism!

All good poetry is the forced constriction of feelings of powerlessness.

Poetry is not the erasure of personality but a caprice of personality. But of course only those who have caprices will know what it means to want to pursue them.

Poetry has as its lower limit insincerity and its upper limit dematerialization.

Use absolutely no word that contributes to the direct sense of a thing seen.

double page spread from *The Nude Formalism*

each poem differently and to play with the formal elements involved.

The first slide shows the format of the book. Bernstein: This is the front title page. Bee: The scale is huge compared to the book. These are the epigraphs from the first page. Maybe the author will tell us what he did. This one is called "Fragments from the Seventeenth Manifesto of Nude Formalism." Bernstein: And I'll read this; it's by Hermes Hermeneutic.

Away with the study of flotation!

Articulation is more than an manner of gritting the pendulum!

Down with all authentic formulations of these theses! Down with Adolescent Sublime! Down with Abstract Confessionalism! Down with Empathic Symbolism! Down with Symbolic Empathism!

All good poetry is the forced constriction of feelings of powerlessness.

Poetry is not the erasure of personality but a caprice of personality. But of course only those who have caprices will know what it means to want to pursue them.

Poetry has as its lower limit insincerity and its upper limit dematerialization.

Use absolutely no word that contributes to the direct sense of a thing seen.

Bee: O.K., so that was the manifesto. It is set in a bold display type and sets the note of the book. On the next page the poem is set in a decorative "Gosh" cursive type and is framed by an ornamental romantic border. The poem is a

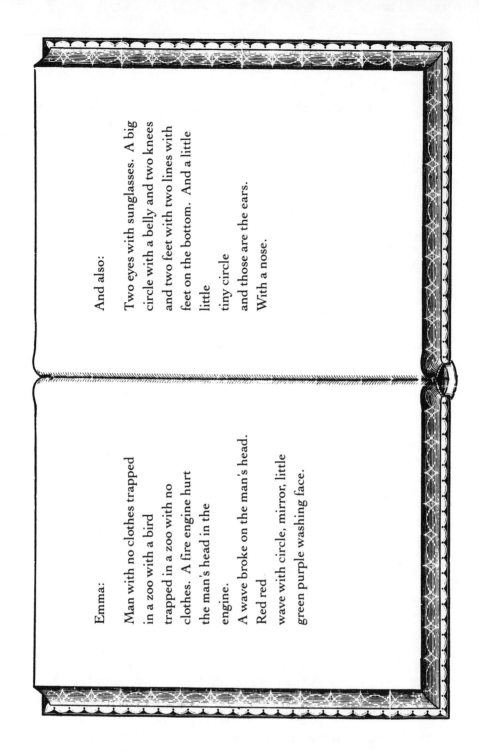

And also:

Two eyes with sunglasses. A big
circle with a belly and two knees
and two feet with two lines with
feet on the bottom. And a little

little

tiny circle

and those are the ears.

With a nose.

Emma:

Man with no clothes trapped
in a zoo with a bird
trapped in a zoo with no
clothes. A fire engine hurt
the man's head in the
engine.
A wave broke on the man's head.
Red red
wave with circle, mirror, little
green purple washing face.

double page spread from *The Nude Formalism*

sonnet that plays in a humorous way with the constraints of the poetic form, including bizarre rhymes such as "thronement" and "cement" and "clang" and "harangue." The archaic, lyric, and the humorous quality of the poem is echoed further by the page layout of the poem.

The next two page spread also involves nineteenth century engravings. The title of the poem is "A Soul, Foiled, Abjured." I chose a picture of souls going up to heaven on the left, as well as an angel for the text. It's in a kind of a wedding invitation font which seems to suit the poem.

Bee: The poem titled "The Cost of Doing Business" is surrounded by two ghoulish, medieval creatures — one holding a stick and the other a bag of coins. I didn't want my designs to be too literal or just illustrative of the poems, but rather to form a counterpoint and setting for the texts. The title, which is a contemporary vernacular phrase, is set in a gothic type. The illustrations suggest a darker undercurrent that runs through the poem and also suggests the yoking of older forms of iconography with extremely contemporary ones which is at the heart of this particular project.

In the center page of *The Nude Formalism* is an inset illustration of a book, opened to its center which forms the border for these poems.

Most poetry books are set in neutral type — so as not to call attention to the graphic elements of the work. In this book, in contrast, we wanted to create a continuing dialogue between the typefaces and the poems. This poem is a villanelle

61

Water Poem

The lakefront view wets
its sea, sanded in beached
out acquiescence; a continueless
(continentless) wading
(blinking)
cast against blatant
horizon on a blue
bloat buoyed by wind and
surf's ripple (forbearance
among) pool-dry thirst:
drowning our tears in liquid
water.

double page spread from *The Nude Formalism*

— a highly structured French form — with the unlikely title of "Ding Dong You're Wrong." It's set in an advertising display font which like the content of the poem marks a sharp contrast from the pastoral origins of this poetic form.

Bernstein: I recently worked extensively with composer Ben Yarmolinsky writing librettos for music theater pieces or operas. It seemed to me in this project especially, as well as others that I have done with Susan, that the relation of the poems to the books is one of setting, much in the way in which Yarmolinsky will set a libretto to music syllable by syllable. I see the typographic and book process as a way of setting the poems. I don't see the poems as existing independently from the setting and so the typography gives the poems a visual meaning that doesn't exist otherwise. This is "Ding Dong You're Wrong" and I dedicated it to President Clinton's rousing visit to the Twin Cities yesterday [April 8, 1994].

President Kennedy's brain is missing!
He dreamed that he was walking in the fields
Mistakes took for purpose, senses steaming

If not IRT, BMT's moving,
    By which to say your plate is sealed
President Kennedy's brain is missing!
As if by chance I fell to stammering
    Kept lush abound my deck, nor grudged me wields
Mistakes took for purpose, senses streaming.

It won't break, it's not yet even speaking
    In one rude clatter done had broke his heel
President Kennedy's brain is missing!

Exulting, trembling, raging, fainting

As slides become slips, necromantic squeals
Mistakes took for purpose, senses steaming

Remote still exaction's circus straining
　　Abbie Hoffman's pain was masked by shields
President Kennedy's brain is missing!
Mistakes took for purpose, senses streaming

Bee: The following poem, "Horses, Necktie, and Water Fountains," is written in a simple, childlike language and is surrounded by an extremely elaborate narrative border with many characters, which alludes to some of the possibilities inherent in the poem.

In the next page an astronomer looks through a telescope to a point outside of the book's margins — while the poem talks of "No way" and "My mind is like a steel trap — once something gets in/It never gets out." The border, however, suggests a possible escape from the page.

"Thrush" is a sestina — a highly constricted French form — often thought of as somewhat frivolous. Here it's set in a decorative script.

The next spread involves more of a Surrealist motif, with an opposition between the poem, "Freud's Butcher" and a tiny bird on the hand.

"Water Poem" has a decorative initial cap with a playful sprite atop it. The poem itself alludes to the ever-present water imagery in the suburban landscape poems of *The New Yorker*. This is all part of the same book, obviously, although it seems like a totally diverse style.

On the following page, the text "Mother, please, I'd

rather do it myself," a line taken from an aspirin ad of the 70s, is framed on a memorial stone and flanked by two women and two babies. Here's an example where the text alone has many possible interpretations but this setting gives a very specific reading not foregrounded in the original.

Bernstein: In the original ad the line was said like this: "Mother, **please**, I'd rather do it **myself**; I'm suffering from tension . . ."

Bee: In the final image from the book, a suited gentleman sprints over the text to vault to the end of the book while staying within the poem's borders.

I'm just going to show one other book that we did together. *Fool's Gold* from Chax Press was done for Charles Alexander in Tucson during a Chax Press Residency in January 1990. In it, a multitude of short texts by Charles Bernstein are set upon and played with by me. This book is in an accordion, long, fold-out format in two colors, black and gold, done on a letterpress. The visual elements are ink and brush drawings and an arrangement of assorted clip art and collage elements. The texts are set in various type sizes and a variety of shapes to complement the visual elements.

This first four pages of the fold-out involve a scissors and a bird as primary elements. One of the lines set is "I'm as nervous as a bear at a square dance," and another is "If you step out a door & there's no floor you may fall & never hit bottom."

Bernstein: Below a crossword puzzle it says "The fact is also a figure of speech as in he cuts quite a figure, or you can figure it out, but I'm getting more dumplings."

The text on the left is like a children's-type text:

Once there was a pobble who had no toes & he had no
name too & he was lying down on a big rock & then
he saw reindeer & then he saw so much he
couldn't believe it. & this is what he saw. He
saw a wizard too. & he saw an astronaut.
& then he saw a policeman who came
by to greet him. & then what he did
was he went back to his office &
then what he did is. & yesterday the last day the policeman said he found a name
that was "flower cloud."
& then what he did
yesterday he found
some toes to
wear.

The poem, "Trill" is printed sideways:

My voice
which last lost
loses lightness.
Lovely to see you
reeling by the
lane you never
made — lovely
to risk
reticence, reverence
recircuit resources
in the wrapped
apricoteries, rusted
edges, succeeding
song.

Bee: The next four pages feature a flying witch, a hand
tossing a ball, a leaf, and some abstract, brush-drawn

elements. I conceived of this book as I would a painting with compositions composed of many elements with the page serving as a blank canvas. Some lines are "let go of your tongue" and "O! O! I'm in an O! tree" — next to the leaf and "You took the mouth right out of my words." The design is meant to complement and emphasize the whimsical humor and exclamatory character of the texts. Thus, the different type styles create a visual counterpoint to the collaged and drawn elements. The words floating, going sideways, and set at right angles, emphasize the nonlinearity of the texts — something particularly unexpected in contrast to the ways in which most poetic texts are organized, in which even the most disparate elements are brought into more uniform visual alignment.

This is the transition between the middle and the end of the book — the last four panels. A prominent line from this section is "Efficiency without reason is desperation." Above this line a couple is boating. Below at the bottom of the page it says in gothic script, "My memory is short, but my anxiety is capacious." I think this sums up much of the feeling of this book.

After the initial sketch was completed, and when it came time to print this book, many additional design decisions were made by the printers, Charles Alexander and Lisa Bowden. So, ultimately, this book became a four-way collaboration. I'm very grateful to them for helping us make this book.

Hyakunin Isshu:
Between Power and Play,
An Anthology in Translation

Toshi Ishihara and Linda Reinfeld

We are interested in the many traditional forms and possible transformations of a medieval Japanese poetry anthology entitled *Hyakunin Isshu,* literally 100 Poets, 100 Poems.

The 100 poems we are talking about today were assembled in 1235 by Sadaie Fujiwara and include poems written over five and a half centuries. The writers whose works are assembled here include emperors and empresses, military officers, priests, women of aristocratic families, servant maids at court, and ordinary people — that is to say, writers from various social classes over a long period of time.

Each verse is in the form of a tanka, that is, a 5 line syllabic form of 31 syllables, 5-7-5, 7-7. The first poem in the anthology as we have it today, shows the two-part structure.

Aki no ta no kariho no iho no toma wo arami
Waga koromode wa tsuyu ni nuretsutsu.

In the fall field, a shelter for the harvest
Dew drips through the weave of the roof, wetting my sleeve.

Verses about love make up about half the collection (43); seasonal songs come next in number (autumn, 16; spring 6; winter 6; summer, 4) and four songs deal with travelling. Parting is a common theme. The collection seems to have been originally commissioned for the purpose of decorating the screens in an elegant summer house. Thus, from the beginning, the collection was designed to exist within a rich visual dimension. In the seventeenth century, the poems developed into a popular card game. This game, with the rules virtually unchanged, continues to be widely played today. The poems, along with their interpretations, are taught in the schools, and there is even a national competition.

In the game, we have two sets of cards. The cards of one set are for the orator, or reader. Each card has one verse printed in its complete form, and it usually includes a drawing of the author wearing the costume indicative of his or her class. The cards of the other set are for the players (usually two, sometimes more) and only the latter half of the verse is printed on this card. The players spread the cards of the second set on the floor. When two players compete, each keeps fifty cards placed neatly in front of him or her. The orator draws a card at random and reads — or chants — one poem aloud.

Oe yama ikuno no michi no tokereba
Mada fumi mo mizu Ama-no-Hashidate

Through Ikuno and over Mount Oe it's a long road, one I don't know
No echoes here of my mother, no word from her home on Ama-no-
    Hashidate

As the orator begins to recite the poem, the players look
for a card that matches the reader's — which means that the
player who has memorized the whole verse can start looking
for the right card without waiting until the orator comes to the
last half of the verse — the part which is written on the player's
cards. The better the player's memory, the better the chance of
winning. When all the cards are taken, the game is over, and
the player with the most cards wins the game.

Card games originated in shell matching. The object of
the game was to compare the beauty of one's shell with that of
one's opponent — winning meant picking the shell judged to
be the most beautiful. And the game of matching shells was
often accompanied by a game of matching verses. In this
version of the game, the object was to come up with the most
beautiful poem. Here the material equivalence of poem and
shell points toward the emptiness of meaning in the word itself
and locates the life or aesthetic value of an object, be it
"natural" or "artificial," in a context created by play. The best
poet is the one who most skillfully selects and assembles the
material available in the language game at hand. Shell cards
with verses written on them were made for those who were not
good at writing poems impromptu.

Although today the game of poetry is usually

considered a-political, for Sadaie the creation of this anthology was not only an exercise of literary skill but a politically subversive act. As a poet who depended for his livelihood and audience on the benevolence of a military government, Sadaie could not afford the luxury of expressing his loyalty to his former patron, Gotoba, now out of power and living in exile. What he could do, though, was use his power as a book artist to translate the values of a disempowered court and courtly culture into a game that could survive in a political atmosphere opposed to those values. Thus the Hyakunin Isshu carries with it a tradition of protest against "official verse culture" and binding authority of the book.

There are two versions of Hyakunin Isshu. Working outside of the mainstream of academic literary criticism, certain independent scholars in Japan — namely Shokichi Oda and Naomichi Hayashyi — have speculated that the anthologies were assembled to serve different purposes. The first version, the one commissioned by the paying patron, does not adhere to a strict chronological order and omits two of the poems. One of the omitted poems was written by Gotoba himself, the emperor who was deposed in his youth and whose court was entirely disempowered by the time Hyakunin was commissioned. The other omitted poem was written by a member of Gotoba's entourage, a woman Sadaie is believed to have been in love with — although of course, given the politics of the time, they would never have been able to engage in an open exchange of letters, let alone maintain a relationship. Perhaps this accounts for the tone of intense longing that characterizes the one poem in the anthology composed by Sadaie himself:

Konu hito wo Matsu-ho no ura no yunagi ni
Yaku ya moshio no mi mo kogaretsutsu

Windless evening. On the shore of Matsuho-no-Ura
They burn seaweed for salt. You're gone. I burn with longing.

The second, more commonly circulated version of the anthology, the one we use today, maintains a strictly chronological order and includes the two poems omitted in the "official" version. It is this "complete" version you see here — rearranged so that the images evoked by the cards combine to create what appears to be a depiction of Gotoba's estate — an image that would display — or should we say, discover? — that landscape of Sadaie's earliest and most joyful poetic associations. Sadaie may have been making it possible for his old friends to read a message he could not directly convey. It is almost as if he was saying that although he had not been willing to give up his public life as a writer and had continued to write poetry even under the Kamakura military regime, his heart and loyalties remained with Gotoba and the culture of the displaced court.

Waga iho wa miyako no tatsumi shika zo sumu
Yo wo Uji yama to hito iu nari.

I live at the high world's border, dragon, snake, and deer
About me, on Ujiyama — sadly, or so some think.

Perhaps as we begin to translate these poems from Japanese to English, we find ourselves faced with a problem analogous to the problem faced by Sadaie himself: how to reinscribe the body of an unfamiliar, old, and perhaps unwelcome language right at the border, the cutting edge, of contemporary American poetry? In the dialogue between card play and computer screen, shell games and trade wars, what is the location of poetic language, the context of meaning? Japanese poetry in English has often been over-aestheticized, romanticized, rendered transparent to an exotic message (a lovely little nothing) always tantalizing just out of reach. Yet for over 1000 years, poetry in Japan has been very much a part of ordinary life. We would like the sense of both power and play restored to this poetry in translation.

It is our project to make these poems available in English in a variety of forms — as material for card games, computer games, and do-it-yourself illustrated anthologies — an example of which we have with us here . . . (I'd love to have permission for a game called "Is that a real poem or did you make it up?" — the object of this would be to assemble pieces of the poems, or lines at random, into interesting combinations . . .)

Originality and authenticity are not our primary concerns. Specifically, by proposing to translate these poems in a multiplicity of forms, we are trying to restore:

    a)   the power of sound in language as the poems are read aloud

    b)   play in language, the drama of game competition

c) language as living material, motion, physical body

d) the visual, the rhythms of calligraphy

e) the image as provocative and political

To make an anthology is to exercise power, to create an order. To take that anthology apart and shuffle the pieces around would seem to break that order apart.

But in the history of this card game, play gradually assumed a didactic purpose, and the cards became tools for teaching. Hyakunin Isshu continues to be taught in school. Students are often asked to memorize these poems — not for the purpose of playing cards, but for didactic reasons: to absorb the principles of literary excellence and interpretation, to acquire a sense of history, to learn what attitudes are considered morally respectable. For our Japanese audience especially, we would like to liberate Hyakunin Isshu from didacticism back to play again.

Even at the simplest levels of the game, where only the pictures are "read," we see the operation of a poetics of power. Children learn how the author's gender and social status control their worth. And in the game as it is traditionally played, read aloud, the first part controls the second part. Language has to be controlled in a rigid pattern of 31 letters. Players have to memorize poems (control language) to win the game. Indeed, the control of language becomes quite literally physical. In the slapping down, moving, and picking up the cards, children learn what it means to take language right into their own hands. With our translations, however, we would like to emphasize the possibility of translation as resistance to power and liberation from control.

Most of our predecessors have tried to keep the number of lines intact, or the number of syllables: some, in an attempt to render the verse in a musical way, added rhyme. We would like to think, however, that translation can be a productive act, writing that liberates text from its original context and opens up the possibility of other meanings in other contexts. The translator, too, is liberated, freed to make the poems rather than receive meanings. Thus we decided to avoid any foot binders in our translation: each poem consists of simply two unrhymed lines. We liberate poems from the constraints of gender by taking the texts away from the authors' pictures. (In the Japanese cards, we see the poets' gender and social status from their costumes and surroundings in their portraits.) This is no small matter. At one point there was actually a deck of cards made with only the women poets rendered in the nude!

We would also like to erase from our attempts at translation the trace of fixed order. Presenting the translated poems in card form is important in that it encourages players to think of poetic material, or material power, in terms of its range and potential for rearrangement. There need not be a fixed context. One can rearrange cards, or change the rules — power, like poetry, can sometimes be played with.

We would like to include photos as part of our own free translation game. Because there is no clear relation between the pictures and the verses, we raise an issue of referentiality/representation. The meaning of the image depends on the viewer. Of course there are editions of *Hyakunin Isshu* illustrated with photographs: they usually present landscapes evoked by the poems and pick up on references to locations, trees, flowers, natural phenomena, etc. On the other hand, in my photos, I cut the direct association between the poems and photos, portrayal and object portrayed. The meaning of the photos is produced by the reader, player, translator. My translation of images can't be authoritative.

Now with the reproduced poems, we challenge the player to assume the role we have assumed, to take over control of the given. Without being subjected to the poems as given, the player poet engages in creating meanings, lists, poems, possibilities. In this way, our translation saves itself from becoming an authoritative text. We don't want any of our poems to be bound within itself. We challenge the notion of fixed meaning, even when it is our own.

We hope to repeat what the great poet did: to translate others' poems and embody resistance, to have texts on cards and shuffle them, to create order by cards and discard it. Thus the player is a translator, destroyer, liberator, gambler, creator, in repetition.

Images From
Pictured Knowledge

Katherine Kuehn

I'm Katherine Kuehn, and I'm a letterpress printer. I'm actually not going to talk about my publishing activities; my presentation would better fit in a category called "the past and beyond." I'm going to talk about a four-volume set of books called *Pictured Knowledge,* published by the Compton-Johnson Company in Chicago, in 1916. This set was found in a local thrift store in Albuquerque by my assistant, and when I looked through it I somehow thought it would suit this panel presentation.

My husband, David Abel, and I have a fairly large collection of commercially produced books that we call our "cool" books, which includes children's books, textbooks, technical manuals, phrase books, all of which serve as a source of inspiration and delight to us. By showing *Pictured Knowledge* to you, I will be presenting the issue of source material and its use by book artists, and my presentation is really dedicated to all those book artists who make use of such materials.

The purpose or aim of *Pictured Knowledge* is stated in the preface: "By clothing the dry bones of the text book with living flesh and blood, by supplying, in pictures and in graphic words, life, color and motion to these catalogs of facts which to the child seem too dry, dreary, dead and pedantic, *Pictured Knowledge* restores the connection between education and the home by a process at once easy, natural and delightful." This new educational approach was an attempt to extend the education children received at home before going to school — when they are learning with their eyes, and where an attentive mother is their teacher. The preface also prophetically states, "The limit and range of what pictures can do is steadily increasing. It would be a curious question for the imaginative mind to work out how far an education based upon a wise selection and proper gradation of pictures might today be carried without the ability to read." These books had over 40 distinguished contributors, of whom John Burroughs, the naturalist, is right in the center. He is profiled in the section called "Some of the World's Helpers," and in this letter he has written to aspiring young naturalists.

As a book artist this set has tremendous appeal for me. For its intended mission or purpose — in what it is attempting to do with text or images, it is a distinctly American cultural artifact and a powerful propaganda tool — and mostly for its bizarre and wonderful text and image juxtaposition. The pictures, which are often fairly mundane photographs, when coupled with some of the captions or text really produce some whoppers. Finding these text-and-image gems is what I love best about the books.

First, we'll take a look at a few pages highlighting the natural world and its wonders. We see here some rather bizarre but terrifically industrious and economical ants. Industry, industriousness and the work ethic might be the most common theme throughout the books. Here, we gaze at distant planets with the hope of someday reaching them, but looking back in time we see — "An early resident of Wyoming" — which the caption strangely suggests we might have seen had we been driving around in our car several million years ago. Visually, I thought this was a particularly beautiful spread, with its contrast of drawing followed by an eccentric attempt to illustrate weather and some of its effects.

Additional visual depictions of weather include "Wild Weather and Art," with Beethoven listening to a storm while, as my husband pointed out, being stone deaf. Here is America as a bird sees it, which I felt might lead to some confusion for a child who might see a bird twenty feet above and imagine that the bird is seeing the entire continent. The text tells us that our continent before Columbus came was "beautiful, wild and lonely, it was stored with a wealth of useful things that had never been used." Things like radium. Here's how a boy from Council Bluffs, Iowa sees America as a continent full of wonderful resources and products being harvested and put to use. Would the girl's view have differed, I wonder?

The extraction and industrial transformation of the earth's riches are covered in several chapters. This chapter on rubber production begins with a fantastic two-page list of all

An Early Resident of Wyoming

In the days when the diplodocus lived in Wyoming a great body of water extended into the land and the diplodocus, like other animals of the reptile family, spent a large part of his time in these waters.

from *Pictured Knowledge*

WILD WEATHER IN ART

© Detroit Publishing Co.

The Coming Storm, by George Inness. (American, b. 1825)

The work of Inness stands in American art where that of Rousseau and Corot does in France. He was a landscape poet. How wonderfully he tells us here of the storm laden atmosphere, the "rolling heaps" and "wild gathering of thunderclouds with their solemn hush before the tempest breaks."

© Taber-Prang Art Publishing Co., Springfield, Mass.

Beethoven Listening to the Storm, by M. Wulff. (German)

Now the storm breaks. As Inness put the poetry of nature on canvas, so Beethoven told of its grandeur in his music. The great word painter, Henry Ward Beecher, has translated both the music and the storm for us into words on the opposite page.

from *Pictured Knowledge*

the stuff made from rubber — from the "one tree that, if hung with its own gifts to us, would make a Christmas tree" — which is really very bizarre. Here we have the great story of oil, and the long strange story of a bucket of coal, where we learn how ancient forests and animals were petrified and reformed expressly for our use as modern fuels. Crops like sugar are cultivated and harvested world-wide to fill our sweet tooth, while at home, Corn is King. This is a particularly interesting chapter highlighting how Uncle Sam decided that "when the boys of today grow up they are going to stay on the farms and double the corn crop." To do this, the government established corn clubs, and held a contest in which 50,000 boys aged 12–16 followed the government's advice and proceeded to grow the best and most corn on one acre of land, thereby establishing a firm relationship and trust between America's young farmers and the government. Here we see two fine American crops: corn and American farm boys.

This set, which was published in Chicago, views the South as a foreign country. Here is a depiction by kindergarten children from Menomonie, Wisconsin. The South is described as a land of gay songs and tunes, a "land of plenty where everyone gets fat or fatter," the land of bright skies, rice, sugar cane and cotton, of "cozy cabins and white pillared plantation houses," of "tinkling banjos and dancing feet." The South was viewed as being quite an exotic place, with some unusual forms of wildlife. The land, however, was happily being transformed from dismal swamp to happy farms, while to the north lies Canada, with this inspiring photo of enviously huge wheat fields. In our island possessions we lent our assistance in the form of agricultural schools, where, we wisely reasoned, "thickly settled as it is, and with all its wealth in the soil, Porto Rico must remain a happy isle of small farms, and simple, contented people." Our attitude toward Panama was far less benign, and this image of two boys with their shovels becomes quite ominous as we read the text: "At the narrow southern end of North America lies a little country that has played a big part in the history of the world. Only forty-seven miles wide at its narrowest point, the Republic of Panama separates the Atlantic from the Pacific Ocean. It lies across a great water trade route like a landslide across a railroad track. Really, it would be more useful if it weren't there, at all!" Of course, we accomplished one of the world's engineering feats in Panama, a feat attained, we are told, by following the strict principles of total absence. These locks included a most wonderful feature, an automatic brain, making it impossible for a lock operator to make a mistake.

Back at home our technical triumphs included the building of enormous ships that, when stood on end, were longer than the 770-foot Woolworth building (which, if built upside down, would not touch the bottom of the channel used to bring water to New York City). Technical developments included the creation of machines to do intricate work. Here we see how a twine binder imitates the motion of a human hand, and the marvelous speed with which machines produce everyday objects. Yet strong, brave men are needed to man the machines, in this instance, New York City subway trains, and

85

to build our skyscrapers, designed by architectural engineers who propose that "there's plenty of ground in the sky!" Certain types of men are needed to do certain types of work, like these heavy men who work in the curing room of a tire factory. Some men do the dangerous work of going into our mines to dig our buried forests, while others fearlessly sit around reading library books while waiting to fight fires. A number of exceptional men are inventors. Here Thomas Edison, looking like Gerard Depardieu, is shown after five sleepless nights and days listening to the first words from his phonograph. Other, even more exceptional men are leaders. Lincoln, the savior of democracy, is portrayed in mythic terms with positive reverence to his trivial habits.

America's great women, of course, include Lincoln's mother: a short-lived, long-suffering woman of high morals and standards. We are told that by dying young she left Lincoln a precious gift, "pity for every helpless, suffering thing." Yecch! Dolly Madison provides quite a different sort of role model. Dolly did not have Mrs. Washington's strong character nor Mrs. Adams's fine mind, rather she was beautiful and knew how to throw a party, and without her, shy James Madison might never have been president. Contemporary career options for women included commercial art. Here we see Miss Betty Harris at work in the art department of *Pictured Knowledge*. And we are told many women are employed as food inspectors. Here we see a woman inspector destroying bad fruit.

Far from the adult world of work are the happy pursuits of childhood, and the numerous and useful activities

If the Liner Stood on End

Courtesy Scientific American. © Munn & Co.

Of course, these giants of the ocean don't stand on end along side of great buildings as one is shown doing here, but only by such comparison can we realize the immense size of modern vessels. The Woolworth Building is 770 feet high, but, as you see, this steamship, which is 919 feet long, would reach about 200 feet higher into the air.

from *Pictured Knowledge*

children can partake in. They can, for instance, go outside and pretend to rake leaves; girls can make lovely and artistic objects, wearing their pristine clothing, while boys can make useful things, simultaneously forming habits of self-reliance, perseverance and thoroughness. And sane Fourth of July celebrations can prevent the fate of the boy on the right, who has celebrated the Fourth in the old-fashioned way with fireworks. At the top right the girls are dressed up as firecrackers, as fireworks, which looks like lots of fun, while on the bottom we see slum children having the same celebration in their way.

Pictured Knowledge proposes innovative ways for children to learn different mathematical concepts: learning about decimals with flower petals, learning fractions with a clock, and learning about percentages by slicing a pie. The domestic science sections shows a young shopper what various cuts of meat should look like. While chopping up animals is presented in a straightforward manner, the functions of the human body are described in an extremely imaginative way. The body's cells are described as "industrious workers" functioning in a commune, each working for the other's welfare and more efficiently than in any factory. The body comes complete with laboratories, assembly lines and libraries, and with a brave staff of policemen whose only job it is to eliminate undesirable foreign elements.

Looking through *Pictured Knowledge* brought me to re-reading a manuscript by my friend, the poet Joe Napora, who has written a long piece called "1917." For Joe, the year we entered World War I was not only the year sauerkraut became Liberty Cabbage, but was a year of draft riots; a year when, if you asked why we should go to war you were answered with a sentence in jail; a time when farmers were forced to buy war bonds and have property confiscated when they refused; the year of the Butte, Montana, mine strike following a fire killing 104 miners; the year of the East St. Louis massacre, one of our country's worst racial bloodlettings; the year of the Wobblies headquarters being raided in Chicago; and the passage of the Espionage act.

The contrast between Joe's manuscript and *Pictured Knowledge* was so striking and full of resonance that it got me to think this was part of what artists and writers and book artists do. We go back and take another look. Every era is one of transition in which we constantly attempt to recreate, reform, renew images of ourselves and our history. This is part of our work, part of the process of putting out into the world a new perspective and a new vision.

So this is just a beginning, my showing you *Pictured Knowledge,* as we hope this gathering is also.

Nexus Press:
A View from the Loading Dock

Jo Anne Paschall

My name is Jo Anne Paschall and I am the director of Nexus Press, a non-profit visual arts press in Atlanta, GA. Contrary to the description mentioned earlier of my beloved Southland as quoted from *Pictured Knowledge,* I'm not a "fat person with dancing feet singing songs of mirth in my white columned press building located in a dismal swamp!" Hopefully, my lecture will dispel some of those humorous stereotypes since I know that it will be impossible for you to ignore my accent!

Nexus Press prints and publishes artists' books. We are primarily an offset facility and the Press staff works in collaboration with artists who are in residence for a month at a time. We are one of four programs of Nexus Contemporary Art Center, the others being a gallery, artist rental studios and a performance art component.

Nexus began as a photography cooperative in 1973 after a group of students from the art department at Georgia

State University in Atlanta experienced the frustration of censorship of their work at the campus gallery. In a salon meeting at the home of one of their professors, they decided to join the numerous other artists in the U.S. who, during that time, decided to take active measures to bypass the existing established venues in place for the presentation of art; the gallery and the museum systems. They formed the Nexus Photographic Cooperative, remodeling a shotgun storefront into a gallery space, and opened the first photography gallery in the Southeast.

The dues that they paid to the collective essentially paid for the rent. They took turns keeping the gallery open. The gallery was an immediate success and enjoyed successful shows because there weren't many photography galleries in the United States at the time. A lot of people from outside of Atlanta were applying to get shows in the Nexus Photography Cooperative Gallery. After a couple of years they wrote a grant proposal to request funding to develop a travelling exhibition of Southern photography, and of course wanted to publish an exhibition catalog to go along with it. Well, the frustrations these 20 to 25 photographers experienced having their photographs printed by a commercial printer in one book led them to decide that they could do it better. Michael Goodman, in particular, and several other artists who were members of the cooperative early on, were concurrently interested in the growing phenomena in the early 70s of integrating their photographs into the narrative sequence of the book format. So, a secondary program was developed for the photo cooperative and that was to print and publish artists' books, that at the time had a very strong photographic bent to them. The one thing they had to do though, was look for a larger space. They found a lot more space than they really needed. It was an old pre-World War I elementary school building. But at the same time, and not just in photography, all sorts of other grass-roots organizations were cropping up in Atlanta. Therefore, a lot of arts groups were looking for space. Many of the different film, video and visual artists were renting the school rooms as studios. It was an incredible coming together of a variety of the arts. The photography cooperative rented only a certain portion of the building, using part for the gallery with room for a press room in the back. And so began Nexus press. All the different organizations maintained separate governments. With the changing of time and with the challenges of non-profit status, a number of these organizations ran their course, moved out, or ended up combining efforts. Eventually, they became one central contemporary arts center that grew out of the little cooperative of the early 70s and it's presently called Nexus Contemporary Arts Center. We lost that space in 1988 to developers and moved to Means Street, one block south of the Georgia Tech campus. Our board launched a capital campaign and we are, in fact, in ownership of the building. Strategically, we only did what we *could* do and decided we weren't going to go into debt. We decided to maintain all four programs that the Contemporary Arts Center had by that point evolved to, which was the Press, a gallery space, artists' studios (which is

93

subsidized rental under market value), and performance space. The Press was the first to make the move to Means Street. We found a lot of kudzu! A nice metaphor for Nexus Press. As we raised the money, the buildings evolved. We tried our best to maintain the inherent integrity and historical characteristics of the buildings. With subsequent fundraising the gallery was able to move in several years after the press. Within another two years, the artists' studios were available and now we're not going to try to convert space but will build a black box that is designed as a performance space. So, that is the last program to be added to the new art center. This is the gallery and it's pretty glitzy, a far cry from the artist-run studios and gallery in the old school space. It's definitely an organization that has grown up. Here are artists studios and courtyards.

I'll talk a little bit about the programs of the Press specifically. The one that we're most known for is our residency program. Annually, we do a mailing on an international scale inviting book or project proposals for any sort of creative alternative use of the offset medium. All sorts of approaches are invited and we select two projects to fund each year. As you can imagine, we're heavily funded through the NEA and other government sources. As we get more experienced, we're better at getting corporate and individual contributions to fund our projects.

As I mentioned before, we're able to do two books a year, including a recent one by Carol Barton, who is a book artist out of the Bethesda, Maryland area. Her work is a pop-up called *Instructions for Assembly*. As you can imagine, we are capable of doing more than two books in a year. So we had to come up with creative financing to figure out other ways to print and publish books. The secondary program was developed, called Artist Initiated Projects. When we get down to bare bones in the selection/editorial process about 30 to 50 books are excellent and should be printed. It's an incredible dilemma to narrow down to two. So, with Artist Initiated Projects, we draw from the same submissions a number of projects that we want to publish, that we are willing to print, but we don't have the funding to buy supplies, so we encourage the artists, by giving them this particular award, to go after funding that we as an institution can't touch. We can only go after certain funding but there is a lot of money out there that we can't go after; it's only available to individuals. By writing letters of support and acknowledging that we will definitely print and publish this book if the funding is available (knock on wood), the majority of the artists who go after the funding get it. That's how we are able to collaborate with the artists to fill out our publishing year.

In addition to our printing efforts we are publishers. We market, distribute, and sell the books, working with the artists on contract basis, to the point of paying royalties for the duration of the life of the edition.

I think the hardest things for Nexus Press to do is to print a catalog of its own work. It's like the cobblers' babies who didn't have shoes — I don't have calling cards nor do we have very many catalogs. The main method by which we sell our books is through direct marketing, each book individually through a card or flier. I find that has worked quite well for Nexus Press. This brings to mind the experience I had when working as an art librarian and developing an artists' book collection for eight years; if I saw a book and held a book, it was sold, I wanted it. They sell themselves. But the hardest thing for Nexus Press is that we're in the Southeast tucked far away from a strong book arts community. I need to get a page of the book out to the world and that's how I came up with the idea of the cards. They are often run on the tail of the same sheet the book itself is run on. People who have purchased books through the card usually make the connection and know that when they get a card from Nexus Press it gives them a strong indication of the touch, taste and smell of the book.

We have a strong allegiance, not just to audience development, but to our educational programs as well, and I think they are very connected. Again, if you see a book, you want it. It has sold itself, you have to have it. So, for Nexus Press to complete the mission of the book, which is to get the book out to the rest of the world, I found we have to be educators as well. Of our educational programs, the one that we're most involved in is our active internship program, and I invite any one who wants to come and spend some time with us to hook into that. Also, I have funding available for the Printer's Devil Program that I developed several years ago, the Nexus Press alternative to graduate school. The program involves two years as a paid apprentice with a benefit package to work and train, and I'm trying to develop professionals to be on *our* side of the collaboration. There just don't seem to be enough off-set printers/book artists/incredibly bright/ wonderful people who want to do this much work. That's why the Printer's Devil Program was devised.

In addition, we do workshops and I started an incredible program that is still going on, to produce books with children in the neighboring public housing development. In fact, the very first public housing development in the United States is our next-door neighbor. It's TECHWOOD Homes, and it was built by FDR during the New Deal. These are books that were produced when I first developed the program. I received a great grant from the Target stores, which give money for family projects. I was able to work with a group of children from the fourth and fifth grades out of the school that's built right in the projects. Essentially these children never leave the projects, their whole world is right there. I paired them one-on-one with, first, a writer for a period of time, then an artist to design the work that they had done. Prior to pairing them with the writers and the artists, I worked with the children one-on-one for about three months, teaching them how to get information and how to make decisions about how to get to what they need. I found out very quickly that this was one of the life lessons they would never have unless it was taught. The librarian in me taught them information storage and retrieval skills.

Aside from our educational programs and our publishing efforts, we do a certain amount of in-house printing for the rest of the art center each year. I would rather do this than a certain amount of commercial work, because the in-

97

house printing projects are generally jobs that are really suited to who we are.

The exhibitions that we organize or facilitate and circulate from time to time are an extension of the educational program. This again is just a pet project of mine. One poster that we did also served as an invitation for a show in Montreal.

Then there are projects that fall in our laps. They are projects that we fit into our busy schedule. We were able to get a little bit of grant money during the Democratic convention, (not this past election, but the one before that). The Democratic convention was in Atlanta, and we were able to select three artists and get them passes to enter the convention for a day. They were to go into the convention, look around, see what they could see, and then come back to the press room. That night we printed a poster in reaction to the convention. While the Democratic Convention was still going on, the posters were plastered all around the town. One of the more elaborate ones was difficult to do overnight because the artists wanted to use metallic ink, but a very beautiful poster came out of the project.

Beyond that I got hooked up with an intern who got me excited about his Architectural Jihad — the Aesthetic Holy Wars. We would print scuzzy posters and then plaster them up all over town to denounce bad architecture that was being built in the city.

On to Nexus present and beyond — this is the current project and it's very, very big. It's a large project for Nexus

Press. What I haven't mentioned is that there's myself and one other person — that's the entire Nexus Press staff. Of course it goes without saying that we have some level of support from the greater art center with writing grants, but everything else is Nexus Press's responsibility. One current work is *Mine Fields* by Bill Burke. We've done two books by Burke, a photographer out of Boston. You may be more familiar with the Burke book that was published in 1987, *I Want to Take Picture*. It was a real blockbuster for Nexus Press. The success almost killed us. I found myself being an order fulfillment officer full-time, and that was really a bore. It *was* a thrill at the same time: we weren't used to that volume of sales! He was in residence for three months doing all of the dark room work himself. At Nexus Press, the artists are encouraged to work at every level, where they are able to manipulate and collaborate directly with the Press staff and use the processes within a fine arts context. He had taken three trips into Southeast Asia and Cambodia and had woven the three into what could be considered a singular fictional journey in this book, although there is no fiction there — it's all very real, it all very much happened. It changed for me and many people how we look at photography and how photography can function in the context of the book format. His journal became the text. On the end sheets you see elements of the text integrated just as scraps out of his journal. Or, more formalistic approaches will show a whole spread, developing page to page relationships. One of my favorite spreads in the whole book is about protection tattoos and amulets.

99

Minefields is the Burke book we are working on currently. I had a fear that we would not be able to surpass nor equal what I felt was an incredible experience and book in *I Want to Take Picture*. But it is absolutely a masterpiece. It's an incredible book and I am thrilled and privileged to be working on it. These are the endsheets for both the front and the back. In this book, Burke reveals more of himself, both visually and through the written word. A stronger acknowledgment is given to the importance of his seeing *Apocalypse Now,* and how it initially led him on a spiritual journey. That's Bill, the second from the left. Again, a lot of these page spreads have changed dramatically since this mock-up was taken. But it starts out in Boston. He equates parallels throughout the book between what's going on in his life in America, and his travels and experiences in other cultures. In this book also the integration of the text is much more dramatic to me — whereas beforehand it was integrated visually through collage. But at the same time, there was a definite story that you read as you followed through the pages of *I Want to Take Picture. Mine Fields* has evolved over a lot longer period (normally artists come in for a month and we work together and if we don't finish it before they leave, then we finish it soon thereafter). We have been working on this book for over two and a half years. It has been able to go through a lot of changes that wouldn't have happened had we knocked it out in a couple of months. Layer after layer has developed over time. He has come, within the past six months, to want to add what he calls a Table of Contents. I don't see it needing that at all and we also feel that numbering the pages would be a real intrusion, so I found that problematic. I see the Table of Contents functioning as an itinerary — it helps you flow and pass through the book: Boston to SouthEast Asia to Cambodia, Cambodia back to Boston. You'll find that in this book, themes are present in the photographs — portraits of people in their place, men with sticks, images of mobility — transportation. In his portraits of women in particular (although he disagrees), I feel like he's really investigating women cross-culturally and analyzing the positions of power or the lack of power they have. In one spread which is actually very benign, he treats women in a very acceptable, straightforward and beautiful manner. Another spread is really the opposite; a Bride who is menacing to me; although she's a bride, the cigarettes that she offers as you go into her wedding are a temptation.

Amputation is a theme throughout all of his work. You'll see images of amputation. Essentially his need for mobility and movement is so essential to him, that the lack of it, it being taken away, is an unthinkable horror. He sees so much of that in his travels. Burke has this need to be in places where he feels very fearful and uncomfortable, and he says he makes his best art when he's frightened and scared. So he's looking for the Khmer Rouge, and by the middle of the book he's finally found them. It's a nightmare. The purpose of the book is not just to raise our consciousness socially, but it does that. Even in the serene scenes in the temple, you know that underneath it all the horror is still there.

One central metaphor is a turning point in the book: the image of a battered woman who is interrogated followed by the images of the temple. There's real resignation here that parallels the resignation Burke feels about going back to Boston to face his life there. Another thing that's so unique about this book is that it's going to have a small inserted journal-styled book. The yellow-ochre leaflet book that's stuck on top of the mock-up here is essentially a singular story that he's isolated and pulled away from the book to function as an allegiance to the journal itself. As I said, there's a stronger integration of the text in this book.

We have a number of artists lined up for future projects. Shelagh Keeley, who is a Canadian artist living in New York, does installations and book works that she treats with very much the same space as a room with a wall. She utilizes large architectural-type gestural drawings of anatomical studies combined with appropriate photographs and integrates them into her picture planes. Shelagh is being considered for a large project that I will discuss later in this lecture.

Leandro Katz is an Argentine who is living in the Lower East Side of Manhattan. I'm very excited about working with Leandro. His projected book in particular has a theme that is very near and dear to me, because I like books about books. So this feeds that need in me. We're going to be doing a book that is borne out of a series of paintings. It's about the Codices that were burned, and it's called, "Libro Quemado": Burnt Book. Back in the 1500's a monk in Mexico burned thousands of Mayan Codices and it was recorded that the people were really embittered and horrified about it. He was actually taken to court over it. This book is going to be in honor of and in memory of those burnt books. By burning the books, the monk meant to destroy a culture and the spirit of a civilization by destroying its recorded history.

Another artist, Judith Anderson, is a graphic designer from Seattle. Judy is going to do a book called *Fragments from the Stacked Deck*. *Stacked Deck* is about the contradictions that she finds in our modern-day society, where we don't worry about all these missing and murdered children in America, we don't worry about the thousands of AmerAsians that the American Navy left behind in the Philippines. She's created a series of drawings, collages, and montages that react to this notion, but what's thrilling to me is that she's going to bring these drawings to the Press. And through the process the drawings will change — they will be transformed into a layered, make-ready style and actually be obscured and made into a deck of cards. We'll be pulling things in and out of the press, often not even changing the colors, just adding different colored inks to the fountain and never cleaning the press for a whole day, but changing colors all day and moving the paper in and out of the press. Nexus Press thinks of the offset press as a large tool!

Leslie Bellavance, of Milwaukee, has also received an Artist Initiated Project grant to do a book called *Half-Life*. In her proposal to us she outlined the project which presents impersonal hard-edged abstractions counterpointed by some sentimental conventions of old photographs.

Danny Tisdale, from New York City is going to be coming to work on a book that's actually a book of documentation — it's an artists' book first but it can also serve as a catalog or book of documentation for an installation that he has entitled *The Last African American.* It's a fictitious story that projects into the future that Danny has written about the last true African American. This person was discovered in California, and then was placed on display. Essentially, it's a take-off on *The Last of the Mohicans,* but the story also reflects on a real situation early in this century in California where they found a Native American named Ishi who they determined was the very last of the Yahi Indians. This Indian was literally brought into a museum and spent the rest of his life on display, literally accessed into the museum collection. Whenever there were exhibits he would be brought out to show, "well here he is, he's the last Indian and these are artifacts from his culture." Danny was really taken with this notion, and he has developed an African American museum where he brings artifacts out of the Black culture objectifying it. It's an amazing examination of Black imaging and how we view the Black culture. And also how the Black culture views itself. So we're going to combine the African American Museum into a book about the Last African American. Artifacts from his museum point to the racism coming to your dining room table on a day-to-day basis, through mass media commercialism. Our society can even reduce an antagonist into a fashion statement. Those are the projects that are coming to Nexus Press.

In addition to the selections that have been made in the past year, I do want to make an exciting announcement: I was officially notified just prior to this conference that the Press will receive substantial assistance from the 1996 Olympics that's going to be held in Atlanta. I wrote the proposal in January 1993 thinking that they'd make this decision and I'd have three years to work on it, so now I have less than two years, because I've just recently been notified. But the wonderful news is that they didn't bat an eye, and they gave me everything that I wanted — that's really remarkable, I'm not used to that at all! I fondly call it the Offset Olympiad. I proposed that I print and publish a book about each of the Olympic rings, with each ring representing a continent on earth. So essentially, I'm in the position now, which is really remarkable, to print and publish a book with an artist from every continent, and I have the funding to do it. So the main thing is squeezing it all in — considering that I have an allegiance to the artists already on deck. The good news is I have plenty of wonderful things to do. I guess I'd better clean up that swamp that I'm working in . . . !

Navigating My Electronic Books

Colette Gaiter

The very first HyperCard book that I made was called *The Pyramid*. The opening screen is the interface for the book. For those of you who aren't familiar with computer terms, "interface" describes how you interact with the computer. So the way that you get into the book, the way you read the book, is through the title screen, which is in the shape of a pyramid. The different components or chapters are placed on the pyramid according to their content. So, you would click on one of those squares. One, for example, would be the one called "Progress," which is on the bottom row. Inside is a little story called "A Tale of Two Willies." Wherever there is a little triangle in the corner of the page, you would click the mouse to continue reading the story. This page is from a 1949 yearbook and the photo is of a black man named Willie Horton who had been beaten by the KKK. The photo and the story were in a chapter called "Race Relations." Then, of course, there's the 1988 Willie Horton. The rest of that piece is about the Bush administration and how they handled the whole Willie Horton affair. There's text from a newspaper article that is skimmed in an animated way on the computer screen. Key words in the text are highlighted to guide the reader along at a fast pace.

One chapter is called "Right There in Black and White." It's basically a little meditation on the meanings of, and the associations we have been trained to have with, the colors black and white — white is good, black is bad. Most of the images are appropriated black and white images. They work really well with HyperCard, which at this time supports only black and white. I use a lot of images from old ads because advertising is such a pervasive and insidiously instructive medium in our culture. It's where we get a lot of our ideas of "how things are supposed to be." I've annotated these ads with my own spin on what's happening in them. The images include one of those black jockey figures white people sometimes have on their front lawns.

In conjunction with my next interactive book, I decided to make an installation. One of the things that is challenging about interactive media is that the medium is unstable. Within the Macintosh environment, there are all kinds of compatibility problems with different kinds of computers, software, etc. One way to control the way that people look at the work is to use the same computer in different exhibition spaces and run the software from its hard drive. As computers become more portable this will become more feasible.

The piece, called *easily remembered/conveniently forgotten* was my personal response to the 1992 celebration of

Columbus's voyage. It was exhibited in September of 1992, and various objects in the installation relate directly to the Quincentennial. There are maritime objects and ship images and allusions. In the corner on a pedestal is a ship motion lamp, to give you that peaceful feeling of traveling along on calm waters to conquer the New World.

Many objects were actually scanned and put in the HyperCard work. So the objects were there — live, in three-dimensional color, and they were there again, flattened in black and white in the book. I wanted to use the seductiveness of aged and nostalgic objects to draw the viewer into the events on the computer. When the objects get scanned into the computer in black and white they're literally and figuratively flattened out — reduced to representations of ideas. So I like it that HyperCard is black and white and flat because you're no longer looking at an object — you're looking at what the object represents, or what the image of the object represents. In finding the objects to use in this exhibition, I was really startled by how much our culture reveres the whole so-called "discovery" and colonization period in America. I mean, it is still largely viewed as a very positive thing and an enormous accomplishment for Western people. So it was really easy to find artifacts that supported those imperialistic ideas. I was trying to get people to look at these objects and ideas a little bit differently. So you could sit down at a hutch, and there were objects in the drawers that related to the piece. So here's some ship wallpaper in the drawer . . .

One of the ideas that I was exploring in the piece is

exactly how "isms" — colonialism, racism, and sexism — get perpetuated in society. During the time when I was working on this piece, the Anita Hill and Clarence Thomas events occurred. At first I didn't want to deal with it — it seemed way too complicated. But then I decided to take it on . . . In these pictures, which are computer-manipulated, I show or suggest some of the possible different ways that people could look at the Hill/Thomas affair from their particular point of view. The images are superimposed combinations of White male/White female/Black male/Black female.

The images on the computer screen are all buttons. When you click on one of them something happens. I used children's alphabet blocks and typewriter keys, keyboards, etc., just to represent the language or the medium of language in our culture. So certain letters on a typewriter keyboard are highlighted and will take you into an animated segment. On the image of the blocks A B C, if you click on A, a child's voice mixed with an adult voice says, "A is for Asexual." If you click on B, you get "B is for Behave," and then "C is for Control." Some buttons just have little snippets of sound and some of them are longer animated pieces with or without sound.

A screen image of a tree with branches and images is a map for some of the segments in the piece and is another type of interface — you can just click on one of the images instead of using the random interface. You see two ship buttons — those will take you to pieces relating to the "discovery." The other images are placed to seduce the reader's curiosity. The image on the top right is of a cat, which represents a segment called "The Eagle and the Cat," about the Anita Hill/Clarence Thomas case. These images are black and white versions of the color images that were framed and mounted on the wall in the installation. For example, in one image an antique engraving of a white woman and a photo of Anita Hill are superimposed on each other. Obviously many white women identified with Anita Hill in this case because of the sexual harassment allegations, so there was a relationship there that was interesting to think about. Another image puts together the faces of Anita Hill and Clarence Thomas.

Still another image presents more children's blocks — rooster, cow, wolf, mouse, jackal. Choosing a particular block brings up the idea that each of these animals has a gender and character association. For example, the jackal is a "bad" animal, so the piece of work that is associated with the jackal is basically about the misbehavior of men. Each of these animals has a gender identity, so the cow is a female, the mouse is a female, the rooster's obviously a male, and the wolf and the jackal are male.

One image dissolves to an engraving — three white gentlemen in a turn-of-the-century scene. The engraving looks absolutely "normal" by our standards, but then it dissolves to another image. This image gives people a bit of a jolt because very few of us realize that there were distinguished black gentlemen in America at the turn of the century because we never hear about them and certainly have not seen pictures of them. So the image is shocking or at least surprising.

There's a very interactive part of the book that's like a

game. You are asked to choose an identity. Your choices are white or black, rich or poor, educated or uneducated, male or female. These are the four major identities that determine pretty much where we go and what we do in our lives. You can try on these identities — there are 16 possible combinations. Once you have an identity, you get your fortune told. You can have your fortune told in the area of money, health, work and personal life. One of the fortune cards reads: "You're often losing the game before you even begin." Another presents a statistic: "80% of Fortune 1000 executives acknowledge that discrimination impedes female employees' progress."

The segment "The Eagle and the Cat" is about the Anita Hill and Clarence Thomas case, and it's a little story that I wrote to make a fable or allegorical tale out of the incident. I think that there's much more to the story than was ever explored by the media. One of the things I was trying to communicate, and to understand myself, was Thomas's behavioral motivations. We don't know with certainty what his personal behavior was. We do know that he was the Black conservative who wanted to be on the Supreme Court, and he was appointed by a conservative Republican administration. This behavior alone is out of character for what we consider to be "usual" behavior for a Black man in politics.

Another animated segment has an image of ships that move across the screen with ocean noises in the background. Text appears occasionally — "friendship," "slaveship" . . . There's text that's taken literally from old history books. One line reads, "In that period, slavery was universal. There was no

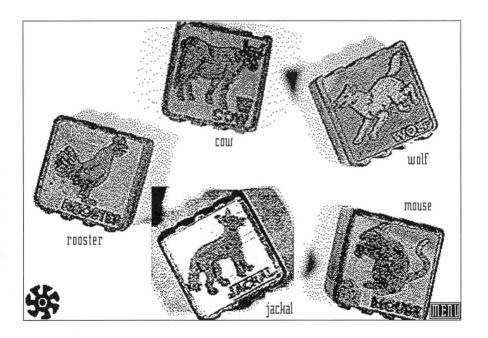

from easily remembered/conveniently forgotten

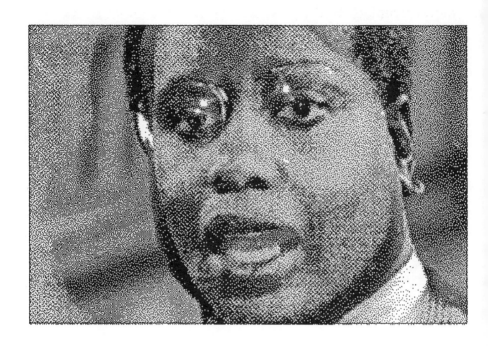

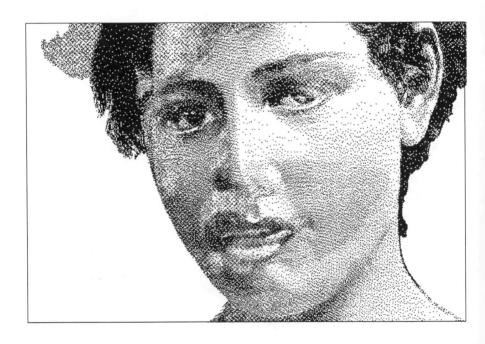

from *easily remembered/conveniently forgotten*

moral scruple as to the presence of slaves." Another reads, "Government promised that the settlers . . . ," referring to government promises to Native Americans about what would happen after the settlers moved on to their land.

There are over a hundred stacks or separate little segments in *easily remembered/conveniently forgotten.* It's a very complex work, and I hope my comments give you an idea of what it looks like and how to get through it. I hope that you'll take the time to go through the work yourselves.

It Really *Is* A Book

Alison Knowles

I'm starting by talking about a book called *Loose Pages,* a human book with human appendage pages; and about a home movie made by Dick Higgins in 1967 in Canada, which was my life construed to be "book-like." I made a book with life-size pages and liveable environments that opened in Toronto. When I perform *Loose Pages,* often with another person, I put her to rest, or, as last night, I let her walk away. I made a book about ten years ago for people without sight that has braille, hieroglyphic, cuneiform, ashanti — many texts which use pictograms to communicate. But the form is intersecting four by five pages, which can be perceived and gone through, in this case with the finger, as in the movie a cohort and I are going through plastics and nylons and tunnels and ladders. One of the interesting things about that first *Big Book* was that the labyrinthine way of going in and around it got me into some trouble sometimes: people began living in it . . . when I got it back to New York City . . . they could actually travel through the tunnels or over the ladders or into the environments and never have to come out. In other words, you could metaphorically, and actually, non-metaphorically, live in a book. It was an apartment which was richly contributed to by twelve or fifteen artists I knew at the time who manipulated an image of a goat. Sometimes it came back in a bottle, sometimes it was just torn apart in pieces. Since it was August we had fans installed in the book — a person could escape from one page to another through a window.

In *The Finger Book*, a finger escapes into the Japanese garden of Ryoanji (a Japanese temple garden in Kyoto with 15 rocks in it). The rocks are replaced with fifteen artifacts from the street: sometimes token buttons, carved. I have a video of a woman — a blind woman actually — reading this book with one finger and singing Indian chants at the same time. Included are Shang poetry, cuneiform, and a Ming arm rest. I discovered at the Metropolitan Museum of Art that many ancient writers would have a wrist rest, so that they wouldn't have to wear themselves out all day and they could rest their wrist periodically before resuming writing. I made a work which goes on a tabletop, a work with Quipu cord language in it, which is a knotted system language used by the Incans to transmit information from one town to another via runners. Since "A" and "E" are musical notes as well as letters, I installed in the *Finger Book* an "E" with a guitar fret and string that could be plucked. And at the end of the *Big Book,* a figure comes out of the window, goes up the ladder (there was an exercise page). Everything was based on really living in the *Big Book*. [Aside from Dick Higgins: "And you made chicken soup there."] Oh yes, I made chicken soup there. And the silkscreen I'm coming out of is the same material that was used to print the pages so that the actual methods of making it were somehow replicated within it. The front page was ice-box doors that had circling lights and the film shows Dick Higgins getting ready to use the chemical toilet.

In a 1983 re-working of the piece called the *Book of Bean,* which had all my Bean information in it as its content, but again, it included curtains, and various ways of getting from one page to another. Rima Gerlovin, a wonderful Russian book artist, turns and goes from one page to another in a black tunnel. A book that's round, transparent, inflatable, and can be read by looking at objects inside rolling around, was part of the *Book of Bean.* The goat and the Meueridge figure are both guardians within the structure of the book. The *Big Book* is a structure in which the spine grips the center pole, which made it very easy to take apart and take to Frankfurt to the Book Messe in 1967. The *Book of Bean* has been performed with Jessica Higgins and a text by George Quasha. Combined with my interest in performance, it always happened that when I showed the *Book of Bean* I would perform out of it. *Gallery in a Hat,* or a *Book in a Hat,* is done by a man named Robert Filliou, who carried his artwork, what he wanted to present to you, on his head. In a work by a woman in Reykjavik, Iceland (I was up there for a week or so), who was confined to her house for a winter, she lined the house with paper, and she looked out the windows on all sides, drawing a line to trace the mountains all the way through the house, and then turned it into a book that fit together so, so beautifully — it was so beautifully crafted. There's sound in the *Book of Bean*. Scott McCarney made a book which is a cut-up of Helen Gardner's *History of Art*. Eduardo Calderón did medicine books on the streets of Peru. You would sit opposite him, and he would find one of the artifacts after he read your aura and give you some way to be cured of some ill. But it was a book for two people to engage in — a performance dialogue. It interests me a lot. The *Book of Bean* has a catalog of books written literally by people named Bean. There was a small library of real books that I researched. I made the second *Big Book (Book of Bean)* with a team of five people and showed it at Franklin Furnace. It was a very exciting summer. The first book-object that I ever made was *The Bean Rolls,* in 1961. It had rolls that were supposed to be used, I think, more or less to keep the book (can) open and around the house. The scrolls came out easily, and you could read one every once in a while. I know my friend Nam June Paik kept his by the toilet and would read one daily. There were also seeds that you could plant inside each bean can. I once ran into an actual bean plant that was grown from a seed in this book. These are things that are "like a bean but not:" teeth and stones and small artifacts on a plate in a small gallery inside the *Book of Bean* and the *Big Book.* I made small galleries to be perceived at eye-level.

A man named Diter Rot made many book experiments. In one, he took the whole *London Times* and made inch cuts, then bound them at the side so he had a small visual book that was as deep as the newspaper. Panels were made in Rochester with people in the Visual Studies Workshop. Fabrics for the *Book of Bean* were from the streets of New York. That August summer we would pick up clothing, old umbrellas, things that we could wash, dip into beeswax, and attach to the panels so the work had an encrusted, waxed, tactile quality. In a drawer of proverbs and sayings we gathered hundreds of quotes, put them on fortune cookie papers, and mixed them with real beans. There's a sound book within the book. It's such a nice text that George Quasha made, as if the book itself is being visited by a Geist and the child, a girl is actually inhabiting the book with an other-voice visitor. When we performed this at the opening people would come out from the tunnel on page three. They could hear things and eat things and, if they liked, go right back into the book again. The scale, the play of scale is nice. I had a dancer visit the *Book of Bean* who walked up the ladder — there was also a ladder in the small *Finger Book*. I had a ladder on the side of page three, so he climbed the ladder and looked around and had a view of this huge book from above. This man climbed the ladder and walked straight over the tops of all the pages, looking down, back and forth, with his arms out like wings — perfectly lovely. Of course who would have the balance to do that?

In one book there are red lentils on a black stocking on a real leg. Actually the portability of these things is very interesting because I can ship them around and meet them, as I will in a little while, I'll meet small books and big books in one place or another. She takes the clothing from the August summer and she examines that. The walking tray was at the exit, and you could feel the beans with your stocking feet. The book includes an image of seven arms on a piece of photographic paper; at the workshop in Rochester, the light was turned on just for a moment and since we all worked on the book all summer we had this form of our hands as a group that was done in a flash. There's the ladder, there's a window, there was also music. I went to the library in Minneapolis and found the work of someone named Barton Appeler Bean who was a great fisherman in the 1900s, and I got all his books and xeroxed his diaries and, using his material to make a series of silkscreen prints and words which we performed as musical pieces at the opening — with people like Daniel Goode. We interpreted the colors and the words of Barton Appeler Bean appropriately at the opening of the *Book of Bean*. I found a book called *Bean Culture* which was adhered to a student's desk full of scientific material. And it really is a book, this particular edition of the *Big Book*. People could spend a lot of time inside. There are many little drawers with things in them and places to sit and look around and there was, as there was in the first book, a kind of *Flair Magazine* extension, so that you could take the page and fold it around yourself and make a triangle within the environment that would intentionally and non-intentionally keep other people and leave you alone with the materials. There are soybeans. There is a silkscreen, and I often do take it off the plate (the printing plate) and make a work of it in itself. Here it is a door. So here you've got a print on vinyl of available soybeans in this country plus a print.

122

There was a bean and barley page, which is red lentils and barley, with a double layer so that it could be sounded by stepping inside. And there were actions you had to do to go through, to go through it — a real action book. As a child I used to swing out over a pond in an old tire — I don't know if anyone else had anything like that when they were learning how to swim.

The Book and The Body: Generation and Re-Generation

Byron Clercx

Although I have never made an editioned
paginated artists' book, I have dismantled a lot of books and
reassembled them into book objects. Over the past three years
I have met scores of others who also make objects from books
or works that employ materials or strategies that address the
conditions of reading. I am specifically interested in works that
metaphorically reference the corporeal aspects of reading.

I met Buzz Spector in 1990 when I was a graduate
student in Fullerton, California. He solidified my intellectual
and emotional concern for works that couple symbolic
materials with specific forms. In Double Readings, Spector's
individually stacked books stand as a measurable and tenuous
matrix merging the physical act of climbing with the spiritual
and intellectual struggle to ascend the corporeal world. Such
building and tearing down in order to build, became the
substance of my works and shaped my thinking about books.

I began by cutting up every book in my possession on a

bandsaw. When I had finished I had a great pile of book chunks but I did not know what, if any, significance it had. I realized I no longer had a library and some of the books I had cut up were my wife's. I had a problem. As I examined these cropped texts, however, I discovered the now displaced portions of text and images were more fertile and interactive than the original texts had ever been. This process of recycling content by physically altering the context of the page was invigorating.

Wishing to make a book for Buzz that embraced his belief that reading is a romantic activity and that, for many of us, the very conditions for reading are intimate, I tried commenting on the conditions or reading. Curled up in a comfortable chair, or in bed, books are close to us; we nestle them and caress them; these are private moments. Aware of Spector's appreciation for Walter Benjamin's *Illuminations* and his own work made from cast glass by the same name, I used glow-in-the-dark lipstick to highlight words, images, and the edges of pages from a cropped text creating poems throughout and a light pun. I speculated that his bedside lamp would kiss the pages while Buzz read and remain as a temporal night light and bookmark while he slept. Clearly, artists who make objects from books, which comment, as physical objects, on books, reading and culture, have been my company and my influences.

Spector's work, *Illuminations,* (glass cast into an open book form), employs the symbolic properties of glass by reminding us that books are illuminating objects. We use glass as a tool, to magnify, clarify, and correct our vision whereby making things previously hidden, visible. This is what books do, of course, or at least what, at their best, they do. Another work that deals with the symbolism of reading is Annette Lemieux's *Domino Theory,* a spiral of books referencing the synapse firing (chemical/electrical) turned chain reaction conceptual process effect of reading with each ensuing book creating the momentum to drive the next one forward and so on.

Books are corporeal in other ways as well, relating to the organic nature of earth's processes. I produced a few early works on this theme by creating machines that ground books into pulp and then spit them into water-filled chambers or by boring rows of holes through dull deficient texts with much the same intent as the farmer who aerates or waters the barren earth, in the hope that something will grow amidst the infertile rows. Scott McCarney's book works deal effectively with this agrarian theme. His piece, *Janson's History of Art* features images cut free from their assigned location flowing loosely across cultures and genders. Another work, *Neverread* (as opposed to *Evergreen*) is an outdoor book installation where the life cycle of the stacked books were amplified by the effects of the elements and animals. Like Doug Beube's, *Sprout Books,* these fertile books have been opened by germination. Here, the act of planting a seed in the earth/book body and planting a metaphoric seed in one's mind by reading, have the same goal — nourishment, one is mental and the other physical.

My pieces then move from the earth to the body more directly, albeit metaphorically. I began to manufacture objects which collate books into a physical form that is used by, or comes in contact with, the human body. Book pages are laminated and carved into shapes that symbolize a text's possible reading(s). Still visible are fragments of text — bits of information hidden in the grain of the tightly compressed pages. For example, *Reading Context* is a life-size chair carved from book pages and newspapers. Power Tool, is carved from Susan Sontag's book *Illness is Metaphor* and *Aids and It's Metaphors*. These pages were shaped into a hammer handle and attached to a hammer head. This subtle displacement is critical because Sontag employs language-as-tool to deconstruct the conventional abstractions used to label people afflicted with an illness and reconstructed healthier, less pejorative ways of engaging the disease. I selected a hammer because of its dual nature, and, like words, it can either build or destroy. Some of my other book-tool-body works include a laminated paper crutch form fashioned from Janson's *History of Art;* a baseball bat titled *Big Stick,* a catcher's chest protector shaped from shredded bibles and self-help books and a cast soap book titled, *Purification,* alluding to the sensuality inherent in bathing and reading. Both are activities we tend to engage in alone, private moments where time is suspended, individual identity is dissolved and we metaphorically leave our body momentarily. I try to construct unsettling objects/ scenarios from well-read books and familiar textual terrain. Bats, hammers, crutches, and chairs are all common objects; tools that, not unlike books, extend one's range beyond the body or support one's position in it.

Ultimately, books, like our bodies, are only containers, yet we spend much of our time preserving and reconditioning them instead of enjoying and sharing the narratives with others. *Freeze Freud,* by Buzz Spector, in part, addresses this preoccupation with climate controlled preservation and ownership. Here volumes of Freud's writings are suspended cryogenically in a freezer, perhaps alluding to the stone age quality of the writing or preserving these seminal works for future generations. Douglas Beube's work, *Projected Histories,* features projected slides of illuminated manuscripts onto his nude body. In one his arms are in the air and the book image seems to emerge out of his belly like entrails or a birthing. Here life and death, body and book coexist.

Examples of books that are symbols for our mortality can be found in most cemeteries. These marble books are often presented in an open and blank format, which I like best. While some interpretations of these marble books refer to 'The Good Book' in a Judeo-Christian context and others function more as symbols for the deceased person's wealth, possessions or knowledge. I prefer to think of the open book form as a more abstract notion, symbolically standing for the unwritten chapters of a person's life, those that are hopefully written in the minds of the survivors. For this reason, I contend that the act of encountering the Vietnam Memorial is akin to reading a book. Like a book, its open walled structure silently welcomes readers to descend into its narrative. Enveloped by the space one is immersed in contemplation, an internal quiet not unlike that found in a library. Rubbings are taken from the engraved names on the wall, like notes from a book, evidence of a body that is no more, but a narrative continually written.

JAB Talk

Brad Freeman

I'm pleased to announce the publication of a new journal, *JAB, The Journal of Artists' Books. JAB* was conceived about two years ago during an artist's residency at NEXUS Press. Johanna and I were there printing a book called *Otherspace: Martian Tylopography.* I am going to read from *JAB, The Journal of Artists' Books.*

This being the inaugural edition of The Journal of Artists' Books, it is appropriate to offer a statement of purpose. Artists' books have come of age. This is increasingly evidenced in the number of mature artists whose primary medium is artists' books, the many public and private collections, exhibitions, college level classes, and texts about artists' books. JAB will be a forum for serious and lively debate about artists' books and the contents within them. Buy more artists' books. They're cheap. They're not cheap. Does Democracy need true fables?

Adolescent George Washington, testosterone brimming to

overflow, chopped down the cherry tree, was found out by his father who squeezed young George until he fessed up. He was man enough to be honest once he was caught and take the consequences for his misdeed. Because of this and a few other moral and manly qualities, George went on to become one of our founding fathers and the first President of the United States. Every school boy knows this. But, guess what? It's all a fable created by a liar. In 1806 Mason Weems wrote a biography of Washington as a scheme to make money. In order to add authority to his tale and put God on his side, Weems attached "parson" in front of his name and invented a non-existent parish.

Janet Zweig's kinetic sculpture *Invention and Revision* (1991) elegantly comments on this tale. On the wall, framed in cherry wood branches, is the famous text by "Parson" Weems. Directly in front of this is a dot matrix printer which prints out the tale at a constant and loud rate. The paper is pulled simultaneously to a paper shredder a couple of yards away and silently shredded into a growing heap. The printer and shredder are both mounted on cherry wood logs. Zweig's piece was first exhibited at PS 1 in Brooklyn in 1991.

In this smart and witty rejection of the patriarchal myth of the founding fathers, Zweig has created a book-like object that really works. On a conceptual level *Invention and Revision* traverses nearly two centuries by exposing the way in which nineteenth century authority (after discovering that it had stumbled upon a lucky bit of propaganda) perpetuated itself on lies all the way to the present era — with the shredding of information belonging to the public and potentially harmful to the careers of public servants doing the deed. Nixon, North, and other flag lovers.

On a formal level how is this a book-like object? Between 1975 and 1989 Zweig made seven editioned artist's books: *Heinz and Judy*, a play, *Sheherezade*, *This Book is Extremely Receptive*, etc., two of which are collaborations with the writer Holly Anderson. These are real books; they have paper pages that turn, they're bound in covers, they're small and portable, they have text and images. Since that time she hasn't "thought in terms of books". Instead, Zweig made a series of static sculptures constructed of books which explored different ways of reading. One of these, *Self Reference* (1990) is a 3½' high cube. An opening in the top allows the viewer to see inside where four shelves of books face one another. These books, spines rigidly toward one another and shut off from the outside world, are a deadpan joke on artwork that refers to itself. This gentle indictment brings to mind books used as props by artists who think the fetishized object itself will bring with it some of the presumed knowledge, prestige, and aura contained in the original. Think of window displays in chic boutiques or a TV interview of some expert authority in front of her/his bookshelf.

What is it about *Invention and Revision* that makes this machine book-like? In fact, what does "book-like" mean and why should we be concerned? Partly because there is an ongoing debate out here in Book Art World about what is and is not a book. Most of the sculpture that purports to be book-like merely refers vaguely to the form of the book without actually having any of the time tested qualities of a book. Merely mimetic devices, they refuse to evolve into viable new forms. They are static one-liner sculpture gags in the shape of books. On the other hand, the meaning within a book is revealed through space and time as the pages are turned. Zweig's hybrid invention dynamically moves paper electromechanically and is programmed to print (!) on paper an appropriated text which is then turned inside out, exposed and deposed. This subversive device has opened new doors in the definition of book-like.

The only problem with *Invention and Revision* is that I can't go to my bookshelf, pull it out, hold it in my hands and read it as with Zweig's books.

Bring Ollie North back for another round.

Invention and Revision was the first in a series of computer driven kinetic sculptures (CDKS) created by Zweig. The second was *The Liar Paradox (Oliver North Mobius)*, also completed in 1991. A liar paradox is one of the earliest classic Greek logic paradoxes. It goes something like this: "I am now lying." How can this make sense? If a person says she/he is lying then are they telling the truth that they are lying? It is a circular self contradiction which goes round and round and nowhere. Recurrent structures are very appealing to Zweig and become a central motif in this next phase of her creative output. For *The Liar Paradox (Oliver North*

Mobius) she took questions and answers from the 1986 Iran/contra senate testimony of Lt. Col. North and put them into a computer macro program. The program has the ability to continually randomize the questions and answers. The computer was then connected to two dot matrix printers with a continuous loop of paper between them. The program tells the second printer to print a random answer. Eventually every question falls with every answer on the paper and the Mobius almost turns black with overprinting the longer the program runs. It almost destroys itself. But not quite. It is a perfect metaphor on the way no intervention was made into the real power of the Reagan administration. The constant flow of red herrings, obfuscation, evasions, and irrelevant counter charges keeps the "enemy" (a.k.a. U.S. citizens) from knowing the truth.

For *Mind Over Matter* (1993, CDKS) Zweig took three famous statements that deal with ontology, existentialist position, and individual will and put them in a randomizing program.

I think therefore I am. -Descartes
I am what I am. -Popeye
I think I can. -the little engine that could

The program takes the three statements and makes combinations of different sentences. The original quotes are essentially positive in their outlook, or, as in the case of Popeye, at least accepting of who he is. However, what is really surprising is that many of the thousands of re-combined sentences contain doubt as to the condition of the speaker, i.e., I think I can think, as if the computer program has humanized them.

In this and in other ways, Zweig challenges and delights the viewer while exploring the possibilities of artificial intelligence in an expanding array of subjects and forms.

Re-Reading the Boundless Book

Karen Wirth

When I first started writing about books I was intrigued by being part of a thoughtful conversation: examining books by artists, reflecting on their ideas, and re-presenting them to a new audience with other ideas. But it was difficult to decide what part of me would be doing the talking in this conversation. As an artist, I consider my role to be a provocateur, to engage the viewer visually and intellectually.

As a teacher my role is similar, to challenge students to see and think and act, first for themselves, and then in order to address their own viewers. As a writer, it seemed less clear what form of address I should take: challenging, predicting, evaluating? When I started writing reviews for the Women's Studio Workshop in New York, I looked to the teaching model as a way to discuss the work in a critically supportive manner. It is as a teacher that I learned how to select a territory, open it up, and guide the students through it. A critical writer can do the same for the reader.

A teacher is also an evaluator of both projects and

progress. This is a difficult and subjective process. Whether critiquing class assignments or reviewing artists' books, comments should be made not to close off possibilities, but to encourage growth. And it is the teacher who knows that it's critical to ask questions, even when there may not be answers; to bring up issues to see what discoveries are made in the ensuing conversation.

So it is from this perspective that I will address some issues of critical writing for the book arts, in order to open up the territory and see where we go.

Artists make books for an infinite number of reasons about an infinite number of subjects. Some call themselves book artists, or visual artists, or concrete poets, but the common meeting place is the book. And each artist sees the "book" in a different way, as the variety of works in this exhibition [*Art & Language: Re-Reading the Boundless Book*] can attest to. With all these variables, the idea of developing a cogent critical discourse seems daunting.

Books can be looked at as a specific discipline with a history that includes cuneiform on clay protobooks, and a future that includes interactive cybertexts. Within the specific discipline, the book is defined by book arts centers such as this one, artists' presses, book collectors and scholars. But cut free from this sympathetic atmosphere, books are often looked at as a peculiar art form that is not quite like anything else — not quite like books from the regular book store, not quite like the art in regular galleries.

When they do make it into museum exhibitions, artists'

books are often relegated to the library, away from the normal viewing traffic patterns, and usually subject to shorter hours than the rest of the museum. Reviews might show up in *Artpapers* from Atlanta, or in the *Northwest Review.* Although the mast head of *Afterimage* lists "photography/ independent film/visual books" as its subjects, the visual books they review seem to be limited to those with photographs accompanying the text.

Occasionally there is a nod from the New York art press when a famous artist in another discipline also publishes a book, which is seen as a novel addendum to the artist's body of work. To go beyond the art press entirely, the artist has to be connected to a famous author, such as Barbara Kruger's collaboration with Stephen King for the book *My Pretty Pony.* Even so, it was the publication party and not the book that was reviewed in *The New Yorker.* (Feb. 27, 1989. p. 27)

When reviewers from outside the field take a stab at it, too often we are given yet another discussion of how to define books, as if there *must* be a universal canon to which we could all adhere. The issues of the work itself are rarely addressed outside of that narrow canon.

Within a field that constantly has to define itself, usually by looking at what has been, what is the present? And what lies ahead? We may look to electronic publishing as one path into the future, but critical writing in that field is also burdened by a rehashing of "What is it?" rather than content.

This month's *Art in America* includes a feature article on the "digital imaging, high-tech printing and interactive video" from the *Iterations* exhibition from Montage '93. Author Anne Barclay Morgan l-i-t-e-ly relates a few of the works to the social issues engaged by the artists, but the article is generally about the effects of technology on art or on the viewer.

There is the ubiquitous reference to Walter Benjamin's *Art in the Age of Mechanical Reproduction:* "the word mechanical can send shivers down our spines, as it seems to threaten our humanness." I've read this many times before; there's too much looking backwards down a narrow tunnel. Ironically, in order to look forward we are asked to look backwards at someone who was looking forward in his own time. Whether it's artists' books or electronic books, this kind of reviewing concentrates on global generalizations of a material or medium rather than the specific ideas and methods of the work itself.

Books *are* part of a specific discipline with its material, technological and conceptual histories. This is rich material to draw from. But they also can be connected to broader contexts-whether in the art world or beyond it. The critical writer can place the book *anywhere* in an infinite number of possible discourses. And just as there are infinite possibilities in placing the object, there are an infinite number of approaches to it.

For example, *Aunt Sallie's Lament,* designed by Claire Van Vliet with text by Margaret Kaufman, is about a quiltmaker sewing her heart into her work. There are two versions. One is a limited edition of 150 copies, letterpress printed on a variety of handmade and commercial papers, hand assembled in a complex, variable concertina binding designed by Hedi Kyle, and housed in a custom-made-to-fit clamshell box by Judi Conant. The varying sizes of cutouts on the pages interrupt our reading of the text, so that when you turn the pages, different parts are hidden and revealed. The course of words is a short history of the relationship, complete with lamentations, and exclamations. With the interconnections between the binding and the reading, there are both physical and textual meanings to decipher. Recently, Chronicle Books of San Francisco published a trade edition of the same book. It is offset printed in bolder colors on shaped pages with a fixed adhesive binding, housed in a two-piece slip case. It is the same text, yet it is not the same text. It no longer has the permutations of reading that we had before, and the physicality has been reduced — we have a wholly different book here.

We could examine quality and the distribution differences from a marketing viewpoint; or we could discuss the layered texts and the multiple non-sequential readings from a linguist's point of view; or we could explore the collaborative process and labor in making the book from a socialist's viewpoint; or we could address the communal nature of quilting bees from a feminist stance. Each of these discussions would invite the reader to not only see the book in a new way, but to examine some broader issues that are raised by the work.

Imagine a Venn diagram, with all the things a book can

be about in one circle, and all the ways of talking about it in the other. The critical writer figuratively spins them around and examines the intersection. The overlap of the subject and the stance allows the writer to be specific within the myriad possibilities; it also encourages the reader to question and challenge, and to develop critical responses.

In order to get beyond "what is it?" the writer takes a position and plays it out. Within the infinite permutations between the writer and the object, it is important to be able to locate the position of the writer. Who is the critic, and what is the critical voice being used? In the past month, I have read a poet who said writers make the best critics, a painter who said artists are the best critics, and an art historian who voted for scholars. In my roles as an artist, a teacher, and a writer, I can see that each voice makes a different contribution. But as a starting point it is necessary to have an informed opinion.

What makes it informed? Art or literary history, the history of the book, the biography of the artist, the contemporary art scene, the current art market, or the canon of the medium; but also the cultural or social context, what's happening in the news, what might happen tomorrow. It is like looking through a variety of filters, each one affecting the meaning of the work. Being informed is about learning, researching and translating.

But there are two parts to that phrase: *informed opinion.* An opinion is a particular voice, where one takes a stand. It is possible to write criticism without the introduction of the very personal voice. But too often the words come from a disembodied voice of authority, while ironically claiming to deconstruct authority. The words author and authority come from the same Latin and Middle French root word, but they mean very different things. The Oxford English Dictionary, which may be *the* most disembodied authority, tells us that an *author* is: *The person who originates or gives existence to anything; the prompter or mover.* This implies forwardness, or creating new thought to advance a position. The dictionary defines an *authority* as: *one who has the power or right to command or give an ultimate decision.* An ultimate or final decision closes off conversation and discussion. And I think it is in conversation that we challenge this field. At this conference, people have presented ideas of books ranging from political tools to interactive communications. Conferences such as this one are part of the educational discussion that expands the genre and its reception.

The questions raised do not need specific answers or solutions — circuitous discussion brings up new questions, and that is how the field grows.

The introduction of electronic books into the schools and the marketplace tells us that the nature of the conversation is rapidly changing. In a recent *Hungry Mind Review*, writer Brigitte Frase develops an intriguing analysis of the printed book compared to the electronic one. She is writing in reference to Richard Lanham's *The Electronic Word: Democracy, Technology, and the Arts* — available in print or on disk (University of Chicago Press). "The printed page, the bound (codex) book with its title and author page, looks authoritative; it can be described as embodying or containing wisdom in a way the unstable electronic text does not." In the multilayered, interactive reading of the hypertext the reader is invited to respond directly to the author, to join in the authorship of a constantly changing text. Notions of author and authority become obsolete. This is the contemporary evolution of the reader/response theory, wherein the reader is a wholly active participant in a two-way transmission of information. We may not be drawn to hypertext, but its existence affects the act of reading all types of books.

Books are an interdisciplinary medium. Meaning is not fixed in material or history or format. The fluid movement of ideas from the maker through the object and its message to the reader, requires open-minded engagement on both ends. We who are artists and writers continue to make and expand the boundless book; we who are readers and viewers are asked to look anew, to re-read the boundless book; and we who are critics and teachers can challenge expectations and act as guides through an ever-changing, and ever-fascinating territory.

Contributors

Dick Higgins is founder, editor, and publisher of Something Else Press in Barrytown, New York. He is creator of intermedia art, and as an artist has been multiply active in literature, music, performance, and visual art. For over thirty years Higgins has been a pioneer in the practice of and thinking about the book arts.

Steven Clay is the director of Granary Books in New York, one of the finest and most influential book art galleries in the country. In addition to mounting exhibitions and hosting a series of lectures, music, performance and literary events, Granary has published more than ten major artist book editions which have involved important artists, writers, typographers and binders in the creation of innovative book forms. Granary Books began its life more than a decade ago in Minneapolis.

Johanna Drucker is an artist, writer and printer who has produced letterpress books experimenting with the visual representation of language through format and typographical design under the Druckwerk imprint since 1972. She is on the faculty of Yale University, where she teaches contemporary art and critical theory.

Charles Bernstein, poet and critic, is Gray Professor of Poetry & Poetics at the State University of New York at Buffalo. Formerly editor of L=A=N=G=U=A=G=E, his several books of poetry include *The Sophist*, *Rough Trade*, and *Dark City*. He has collaborated with Susan Bee and others on various book arts projects.

Amos Paul Kennedy, Jr., founder of Jubilee Press, is a printer and book artist committed to the social and political possibilities for the book arts. Kennedy maintains a strong commitment to publishing African-American histories and narratives. He creates objects that combine craft, spirit, and concern for his fellows. He has involved children in the creation of book arts works in projects throughout the midwest.

Susan Bee is a visual artist who exhibits widely and who has collaborated with several poets and presses on the design and illustration of literary books. She edits M=E=A=N=I=N=G, an innovative journal concerned with meaning and the visual arts.

Toshi Ishihara is a poet and scholar in Japan who is currently working with Linda Reinfeld on translations of Japanese poems. She received her Ph.D. from SUNY, Buffalo. Her boundary breaking work, *Ran's Notebook and Drawing Book: Speculations by a Japanese Woman on Cultural Differences*, is a configuration of autobiography, (de-)critical feminist writing, love letters, and poems.

Linda Reinfeld is an independent scholar and poet living in Rochester, New York. Her book, *Language Poetry: Writing as Rescue*, explores the relationship between contemporary American poetry and critical theory. Her essays and poems have appeared in a number of magazines. Currently, she is teaching at Monroe Community College, exploring the Internet for its poetic potential, and collaborating with Toshi Ishihara on translations of Japanese poetry.

Katherine Kuehn holds an MFA in printmaking from the University of Wisconsin-Madison, where she studied in the book arts under Walter Hamady. As founder and director of the Salient Seedling Press, she has been active in expanding conceptions of the fine print letterpress book, especially in the use of alternative printmaking methods in such books. She lives in Albuquerque, New Mexico, and is a frequent collaborator with presses and book artists across the nation.

Jo Anne Paschall is the director of Nexus Press in Atlanta, one of the nation's premier organizations dedicated to the production of artist's books.

Colette Gaiter earned her BFA at Carnegie-Mellon University and is an Associate Professor at the Minneapolis College of Art and Design, Design Division. She has worked professionally in computer graphics for twelve years and has taught computer graphics at MCAD since 1986. As a visual artist, she uses interactive multi-media to communicate her personal view of societal issues.

Alison Knowles, founding member of Fluxus, is a visual and performance artist whose works include sound pieces, radio shows, installations, and bookworks. Known for her innovative work with organic and discarded materials, and for the conceptual rigor of her performances, Knowles has created a number of trans-environmental, full scale, transportable installation works.

Byron Clercx received his MFA at California State University-Fullerton. He has exhibited his three dimensional book works nationally and internationally. Clercx is a sculptor who reconfigures found texts into familiar objects that couple reading with corporeal activity. Clercx is currently Assistant Professor of Studio Art at the University of Idaho-Moscow.

Brad Freeman is a book artist and offset printer with an MFA from University of the Arts. He has printed his own and other artist's books at Pyramid/Atlantic and other book arts studios. Recently he curated the exhibition Offset, which is the first large-scale exhibition of artist's books which explore offset printing technologies. He is on the faculty at the State University of New York at Purchase.

Karen Wirth holds an MFA from the University of Minnesota. She has received two Jerome/MCBA Book Arts Fellowships, as well as a Bush Artist Fellowship. Wirth is trained in traditional and nontraditional disciplines of book construction and has been teaching for almost 20 years. She has exhibited sculptural books internationally. Wirth also writes book arts criticism for Women's Studio Workshop in New York.

Charles Alexander is a poet, writer, and publisher of literature, as well as a creator of fine book arts editions of innovative literary works. He is the director of Chax Press, which publishes contemporary innovative writing in trade editions as well as book arts editions. He is a former director of Minnesota Center for Book Arts.